AMAZING STORIES

FRANCES BARKLEY

Eighteenth-century Seafarer

CATHY CONVERSE

Heritage House Publishing Company Ltd.
heritagehouse.ca

Cataloguing information available from Library and Archives Canada
978-1-77203-441-7 (paperback)
978-1-77203-442-2 (e-book)

Edited by Nandini Thaker
Typesetting by Kimiko Fraser
Cover image by Kimiko Fraser
Map on p. 10 by John Cary, with edits by Kimiko Fraser.
Geographicus Rare Antique Maps. PD-ART/PD-OLD-100

The interior of this book was produced on 100% post-consumer paper, processed chlorine free, and printed with vegetable-based inks.

Heritage House gratefully acknowledges that the land on which we live and work is within the traditional territories of the Lkwungen (Esquimalt and Songhees), Malahat, Pacheedaht, Scia'new, T'Sou-ke, and w̱SÁNEĆ (Pauquachin, Tsartlip, Tsawout, Tseycum) Peoples.

We acknowledge the financial support of the Government of Canada through the Canada Book Fund (CBF) and the Canada Council for the Arts, and the Province of British Columbia through the British Columbia Arts Council and the Book Publishing Tax Credit.

27 26 25 24 23   1 2 3 4 5

Printed in Canada

*To Captain B., MM FNI, third generation
seafarer who shared with me the
secrets, wiles, and beauty of the sea and
Matt, Lt(N), fifth generation seafarer
to whom the mantle has now been passed*

Contents

Author's Note

THIS BOOK IS a work of creative non-fiction about a remarkable woman, Frances Barkley, who sailed around the world with her husband, Captain Charles Barkley, aboard his ship on a trading mission during the years 1786 to 1794. When Frances was approaching her seventh decade, at the behest of her daughter, she put pen to paper and wrote down what she could remember of her life with her husband in the merchant sea trade. She left a small journal that she titled *Reminiscences*, now housed in the British Columbia Archives. During the eight years she spent at sea she had jotted down notes of her impressions and happenings, although she stated that she never kept a journal. Those original notes or diary went missing sometime between 1909 and 1919. The fact that they existed has been attested to by family members who remembered reading it. Captain John Thomas Walbran, while working for the British Columbia lighthouse, buoy and fisheries service, was reported to have used the diary to write an account of the Barkleys' voyage aboard the *Imperial Eagle* for the Victoria *Colonist* in March 1901.

Since the first edition of *The Remarkable World of Frances Barkley*, written by Beth Hill in 1978, and the second edition by Beth and me in 2003, the families of both the Trevors and Barkleys have searched extensively for the original diary, and still it has not surfaced. I think it is safe to say the family story of its loss in a house fire in Westholme on Vancouver Island in 1909 probably rings true. At this point, however, with the thorough work that has been done by family members on the Barkleys and Trevors and their communication amongst each another, there is now sufficient information about Frances and Charles Barkley's time at sea that the original diary is not critical in retracing their history.

This book is based on Frances Barkley's *Reminiscences*. I have presented the facts as they are but have endeavoured to create a more immersive experience while maintaining her original intent. This story is thus a mixture of Frances's words as well as mine. At times there were gaps in Frances's reminiscences, but through research, talking to marine historians and ships masters, as well as communicating with relatives, I was able to fill in some of those holes to provide a more detailed description of their travels. For example, when her daughter died at sea and had to be buried in "Celebes" (Sulawesi, Indonesia), there was no mention of the exact location she was laid to rest. However, looking over charts of the time and reading ocean depths, I was able to determine approximately where they anchored. In another example, Frances's relatives tell stories they say were relayed to them by her of being captured by pirates somewhere in the South China Sea, but she mentions none of this in her writing. It is not hard to guess where and what might have happened, and so I have woven this experience into her story. Suffice it to say, her red hair played an important part in their escape.

Note on Language
I have used place names and their spellings that Frances employed to maintain authenticity but have added a glossary indicating the current nomenclature (see page 132).

Introduction

OVER TWO HUNDRED years ago, Frances Barkley, a seventeen-year-old girl fresh out of a convent school in France, met a twenty-six-year-old sea captain, fell deeply in love, and after a courtship of only six weeks, married him. Five weeks later, she stepped aboard his ship, the twenty-gun, 400-ton, three-masted sailing ship called the *Imperial Eagle*, to set sail on an eight-year voyage that would take them around the world twice. She faced many dangers during her travels, but she was adaptable and spirited and took every challenge in her stride.

Frances Barkley's story is a remarkable one; it is one born of discovery, of firsts, of hardship, of disease, of illness, and of death. Relying on her strength of character and wit, this young woman survived fierce seas that have taken many to a watery grave, shipwreck, capture by pirates, and imprisonment by enemy forces during war. And when life seemed as if it could not be more distressing, she was thrown into an inferno of deceit and of betrayal. Yet her journey is also one of beauty, of wonder, of joy, and of love—a love so great that this young girl would leave the comfort and security of her home and family to follow a man whom she barely knew around the world on a very perilous voyage.

Captain Charles William Barkley was a merchant mariner who sailed the world between 1786 to 1794, trading in sea otter pelts,

Chinese tea, silk, porcelain, and cotton.[1] Although there were many ships in the merchant sea trade, few by the time the Barkleys set sail had voyaged around the world. It was a risky and expensive undertaking, but if successful, merchant sea traders could make a great deal of money. Captain James Cook was reported to have made a profit of 1800% on the sale of three hundred otter pelts that he picked up in the Pacific Northwest. Unfortunately, the Barkleys did not fare well, their hopes and fortunes dashed on the vagaries of life.

By journey's end, Frances had become the first woman to openly circumnavigate the world.[2] She was also the first European woman to visit the Pacific Northwest and the Hawaiian Archipelago, as well as the islands and continents that are the footprints of the North Pacific. During their voyage to Nootka Sound, they were the first of the non-Indigenous explorers to chart what became known as Barkley Sound. The reminders of their visit are still there: printed on all nautical charts of the area are Loudoun Channel and Imperial Eagle Channel, named for their ship; Trevor Channel is based on Frances's birth name; and Cape Beale was named after the ship's purser who was killed on a trading expedition up the coast.[3]

Sailing farther down the coast the Barkleys had rediscovered the Strait of Juan de Fuca, an important finding for merchant sea traders and explorers. For over two hundred years, many had been searching for such a strait that might offer a shorter passage to the rich markets in Asia. The first recorded story of such a strait in European literature was in the 1590s when Apóstolos Valerianos, known as Juan de Fuca, was sailing under the direction of Spain in search of the Strait of Anian. Although he failed in his attempt, he entered an inlet that became known as Fuca's Strait. Unfortunately, documented evidence of this discovery was never found and was subsequently discounted, but the idea of the strait persisted. Then, on March 2, 1778, Captain Cook sailed past the entrance to the strait, but due to foul weather and poor visibility did not recognize that the cape he saw was the entrance to Fuca's Strait. The idea that such a strait existed was all but relegated to the dustbin of illusion— until Captain Barkley's sighting.

Despite their findings, the Barkleys were largely bypassed by historians as they left no published account of their life at sea, and Captain Barkley's charts with his notations, along with his ship's logs and expensive navigation equipment, were misappropriated; his exploits and discoveries were claimed by Captain John Meares. Perhaps hoping to bring some honour back to her late husband, in 1836, at sixty-six years of age, Frances Barkley began writing the story of their years at sea.

It is impossible to know how Frances felt about the people she enountered as she never voiced her opinion in her journal or letters. She did think some customs odd, not so much because she believed herself superior but more because they were foreign to her. Likewise, many of those she met thought her strange. She had great respect for Kamehameha and Chief Maquinna and knew the value of diplomacy. At the same time, during her many stays in Mauritius, an important port for the slave trade, she never once mentioned the stratified society in which white French settlers held the power and wealth while much of the population were lower status Black people and others from the Indian Ocean basin.

It is important to acknowledge that while the Barkleys were not directly involved in colonizing the land and peoples of any of the places they visited, they likely held colonial biases and definitely benefitted from colonial activities, especially as intertwined as their paths were with the British East India Company.

Prologue

IN HER HOME in Upper Clapton, England, seated in a small chair made of the finest Malaccan cane, sits a woman who appears to be of little consequence. Her hair, snowy-grey, is pulled off her face and swept into a voluminous bun, which when the light catches it reveals wisps of golden red threads echoing a time when youth bloomed brightly. In her hand is a fountain pen that she periodically dips into the pot of ink on the desk before her before scribbling down a few more words in a pretty marble-paper-covered notebook. As she slowly fills the pages, one thought at a time, she pauses every so often and runs her hand over the curved arm of the chair as if stroking it will bring back that elusive thought just out of her reach. It is a comfortable chair, delicate but strong, an item she and her husband had purchased during their first trip to Canton in 1787. The words *Imperial Eagle*, Macau, Cochinchina, Whampoa, and Canton appear on the pages, along with the date of the purchase of the chair. November 1787 was the time when she and her husband were sailing the South China Sea. Captain Barkley was in command of the *Imperial Eagle* and was bringing the furs he and his crew had obtained in Nootka Sound to trade for silk, tea, and porcelain in China, which were in great demand in London. England had gone mad for all things Chinese

The Barkley Chair, 1787. COURTESY OF MUSEUM
OF VANCOUVER COLLECTION H976 35 50

and couldn't get enough of the exotic items brought back on these large British East Indiamen.

Thinking back on that time brings up the memory of the occasion when the *Imperial Eagle* first sailed into the Portuguese colony of Macau. The harbour was crowded with squared looking Junks intertwined with large merchant ships flying flags from Spain, Britain, America, France, Austria, Portugal, and the Netherlands, all waiting their turn for a pilot to guide them up the Pearl River to the trading houses in Whampoa and Canton. The view on shore was inviting. Etched into the curve of the bay was the Praia Grande, the main promenade, graced by stately English houses with their large verandas and colonnades, the governor's palace and custom house, Portuguese churches, and Chinese temples. It

Praia Granda, Macao, 1843, by Thomas Allom. PD-ART/PD-OLD-100

was urban, modern, and fresh. Frances knew she would be comfortable in the lovely home provided to them by Mr. Cummings, a supercargo with the British East India Company, while her husband traded up the river. Foreign women were forbidden to go beyond Macau. China held foreigners in contempt and minimized contact. The trade items these Europeans barbarians brought to their shores made the locals rich and so they were tolerated, but the Chinese set the trading rules to their advantage by creating a massive snarl of expensive, bureaucratic procedures. In any case, Macau allowed Frances to enjoy life ashore and to take advantage of simple pleasures, like attending to her personal grooming, enjoying afternoon teas, and luxuriating in the liquidity of time unbound by the demands of the sea.

The chair belonged to her beloved husband and held many memories for her. It had travelled with them throughout all their years at sea, and it was where Captain Barkley would command the ship's business. Although Frances had been widowed for four years, the pain of loss still wrapped its grief-filled tentacles around her heart, at times leaving her breathless. Perhaps writing her memoirs from that chair brought her some comfort. The chair became a cherished heirloom and stayed in the family for 174 years. Then, in 2015, a great-great-grandson presented it to the High Commissioner for Canada in London, and once again the chair found its way on one last ocean voyage, after which it was donated to the City of Vancouver Archives. It is now preserved and protected within a plate-glass box for others to look at and wonder who the owners were and why it seems important enough to be kept there. For it too, while lovely, appears unassuming and inconsequential.

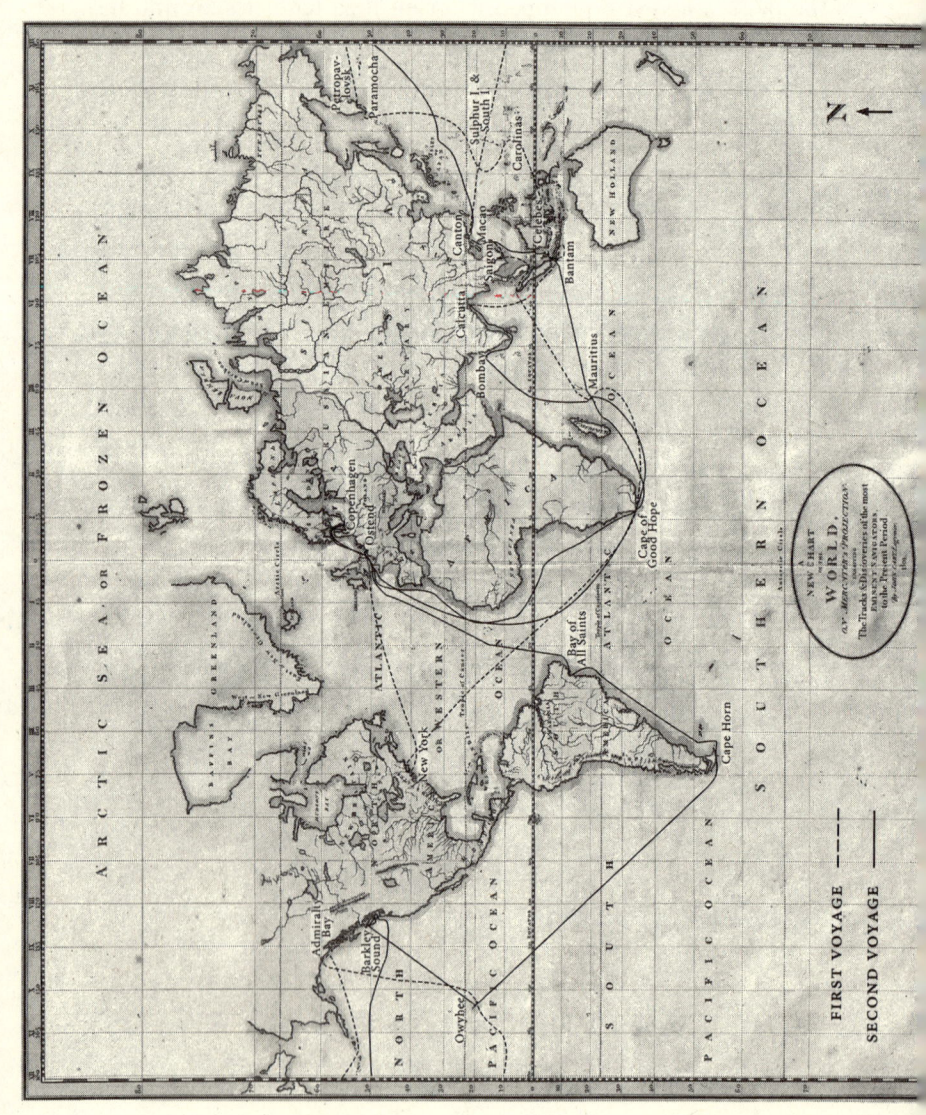

PART I

NEW ADVENTURES

FIRST VOYAGE, NOVEMBER 1786 TO AUGUST 1790

1

Captain Charles Barkley, May 2, in the Year 1836

IT HAS BEEN well over forty years since I was last at sea and some details are shaded, lost in the detritus of life, whereas others are permanently stitched into the fabric of time. I could look to log-books and sea journals to aid me, but I no longer have the courage or energy to pursue them. It is too late in the day for such research. So, where do I begin? Perhaps just a short introduction. It would be tedious to discuss all the stages of my early life. Suffice it to say I was born in 1769 at Bridgwater in Somersetshire. I never knew my mother for she died when I was an infant, as did my twin sister. My father, the Reverend Doctor John Trevor, was Rector of Otter-hampton, in the county of Somerset, Southwest England. He was a restless man who loved fashion and comfort. He indulged his passion with a flourish and spent a vast fortune doing so. He eventually remarried and our family grew, but my father found it hard to settle, which may have contributed to the eventual dissolution of that marriage. We moved many times when I was a youngster. We lived in Rotterdam, Hamburg, and in the city of Ostend, a major

Captain Charles Barkley, May 2, in the Year 1836

Reverend John Trevor. PUBLIC DOMAIN

seaport on the North Sea located in Western Flanders. For part of my education, I was sent to a Roman Catholic convent school on the continent and excelled at French language, history, and culture. When I was seventeen, I rejoined my father in Ostend. I loved living in the city. It was vibrant and exciting. The harbour was always filled with the great ships of the world, stopping in to unload their wares. I did not frequent the docks, but I always wondered what stories and discoveries were held within the confines of those enormous teak hulls.

Although I was now considered a woman, I had not thought much about marriage, but that quickly changed when I was

Captain Charles Barkley, n.d. PD-OLD-100,
COURTESY OF PHIL AND HELEN BROOMFIELD

introduced to a very handsome ship's master, Captain Charles William Barkley, Esq. He was with the honourable East India Company; well born, and a gentleman of manners and intelligence. His father before him was also a master in the British East India Company.[1] My husband had entered the merchant service when he was eleven years old and worked his way up to eventually becoming captain of his own ship. He was a composed sort of person and carried the weight of his command with an air of confidence. There was a natural fit between us, and our love for each other quickly blossomed. Eventually my beloved asked my father for permission to marry me. He was only in port for six weeks, so on October 17, 1786, he being twenty-six and I in my seventeenth year, we were married in the Protestant chapel to which

A British East Indiaman, 1770s, by Francis Swaine. PD-OLD-100. PUBLIC DOMAIN

my father was minister, and by whom the marriage ceremony was performed. Thirty-nine days later, at exactly 1:30 on the twenty-fourth day of November, we set sail on a voyage to places few had ever heard of. I had no idea what to expect. I had only been on a ship once before, during one of our family's moves to the continent. As we let go of the mooring lines, I was both excited for the adventure that lay before us and sad, for I knew that it would be a very long time before I saw my family again. I stood at the railing watching first the people and then the land slowly fade into the distance as the tide carried us toward the great rolling waves of the open ocean.

Some of my grandchildren have asked me why I would go on such a voyage. I admit I was quite naive, but I did not want to be separated from my dear husband. Who knew how long he would be gone, and if something happened to him, I might never find out. Also, he had just left the employ of the East India Company and joined a private syndicate operating under the Austrian flag. At the time, I did not quite understand what that meant. This was to be our first mistake, of which I shall write more later. In any case, our backers were not keen on investing in the fur trade as it was not yet a well-established industry. It was viewed as risky and the benefits unknown. We were in the vanguard of the sea otter trade, so it was left to my husband to provision the ship, a costly venture. Captains' wives often lived ashore, supported by their husbands, but our finances would not allow for that. I would not have countenanced such a thought, in any case. I loved my husband and did not wish to be separated from him.

The *Imperial Eagle* was a beautiful ship, a masterpiece of craftsmanship. Our cabin was located at the stern of the ship, just below the bridge. While it was not large, it was more spacious than I imagined it to be. The large sweep of the windows aft allowed light into our cabin and gave my husband a continuous view of the sea conditions. The stern was the most stable part of the ship and, as I was to learn, quieter than being forward, where the constant crashing of the bow against the waves was both boisterous and noisy. For those prone to seasickness, which I fortunately was not, it was not where you wanted to be. Before we left, I was introduced to the ship's officers, but there was something unsettling about the first officer, Henry Folger. I did not trust him and made a note to myself to stay clear of him.

I met my first challenge at sea three days out. As we were approaching the Bay of Biscay, the sky began to darken, and the wind freshen. The crew reefed the sails,[2] and the topgallant masts were struck. They had to get the weight down as low as possible for stability. Everything that could move was battened down. Captain Barkley, as I sometimes prefer to refer to him in these notes, sent me to our cabin as we were in for some very bad weather. Very quickly the seas steepened, and the wind howled, causing the ship to groan and screech. Together with the clanking of the chain pumps, it all made for a thunderous timbre that was deafening. Our grand ship suddenly seemed so small set against the breadth and ferocity of the ocean. The waves heaped up until they towered over us like tall mountains. We struggled to reach each crest hoping the wave would not break and crush us with its frothy angry power. We then hovered on the summit, momentarily balanced in some death-defying feint, and then fell uncontrollably into the trough on the other side. This went on hour after hour, but each time the *Imperial Eagle* simply shuddered and rose to the challenge of the next wave. It was as if the sea was shaking its brawny fist at us to remind that it reigned supreme. This was the most frightening thing I had ever experienced in my life, but I would keep that to myself. Captain Barkley had enough to contend with. In the aftermath, as I walked the decks, a scene of devastation was laid out before me. Our masts and spars were still intact, but all our livestock was gone. In the chaos, our ducks, chickens, and turkeys had been washed overboard. This, I was to learn, would not be the last of such events; there would be many more and much worse.

My dear husband suffered a terrible chill during the storm, and it was shortly after that he caught a violent cold and was laid up with rheumatic fever. I feared he would not recover. I ministered to him as best I could and made a mixture of laudanum, camphorated spirits, ginger, and capsicum, hoping to purge the sickness from him.[3] It was during this time that the chief mate, supported by the second mate, made unwarranted advances toward me. I had always felt that Mr. Folger was unprincipled, but I was shocked at Mr. Miller as he was a Lieutenant in His Majesty's Service and ought to have had more honour. I dare not think what would have happened had my dear husband not survived. I resolved not to mention any of this to him.

We were now six weeks into our voyage and heading for the Portuguese colony of Brazil. Captain Barkley, although now able to resume his duties as master of the ship, was still weak from his illness and was looking forward to rest and to replenish our ships stores. The weather was much calmer now and one particularly pleasant afternoon we spied a friendly ship. They hailed us with their signal flags indicating they wanted to come near to speak ship. It was a welcomed opportunity to exchange information with them about weather and points of navigation, which we would then each be able relay to the backers of our ships once we entered port. They were from Baltimore and headed for the Cape of Good Hope. After a short time, and with the deft handling of the helmsman, we wished them good fortune and went our separate ways.

2

Recuperation in Brazil

IN DUE TIME, we sighted the entrance to the Bay of All Saints and the order was given to ready the ship. A ship's arrival was always a cause of celebration, and the officers and crew were resplendent in their matching uniforms, all standing at attention, when we sailed into the port city of Salvador. However, with our twenty guns and our formality, we were initially mistaken for a King's sloop-of-war. The Portuguese authorities viewed us as a hostile force and prepared to seize our ship. Tension gripped our crew, but as we drew closer, the Portuguese realized we were a ship on a voyage of trade and greeted us with great ceremony.

I was young and inexperienced and did not understand the grand festivities that took place aboard visiting ships. As Captain Barkley was still weak, I was given to act as his ambassador visiting dignitaries ashore. For these events, I dressed in my finest and was accompanied by Mr. Miller, who in his naval uniform cut a dash. When my husband was fully recovered it became our turn to entertain. Our first visitors aboard were the viceroy and his wife,

Lady Donna Marie, and their little daughter, along with a complement of officers and others whose positions I did not know. For the
occasion, the yards were manned, and the *Imperial Eagle* was fully
dressed, flying the colours of all nations. It was a magnificent view
to behold. When the viceroy drew near, the *Imperial Eagle* fired
a salute in honour of their boarding. We had the most wonderful
fête, and I welcomed the opportunity to talk to other women, particularly as they spoke French, for at the time I did not understand
Portuguese. During these visits, Captain Barkley was quite gre-
garious and loved nothing better than to entertain. He was proud
to show his ship. Having been a master with the British East India
Company, he was well trained in protocol and etiquette. On the
sea, Captain Barkley was a martinet. He was a strict disciplinarian
and demanded immediate compliance with his orders. He never
raised his voice, but when he gave a command, he would square
himself and speak firmly and with authority. He treated his crew
well and was respected by them, but you dared not challenge him,
for doing so could put the ship and crew in danger. The chain of
command is very important for the safe operation of a ship. Only
once did he have occasion to have a sailor whipped. The miscreant
received a dozen lashes for insolence.

CHAPTER

3

Around
Cape Horn

WE SPENT MORE than a month in port, then on February 7, the
order was given to weigh anchor. We left with the outgoing tide,
and once out of the bay we picked up a moderate breeze and turned
south toward Cape Horn. I had heard worrying stories about this
leg of our journey. It is a notorious piece of water beset by strong
currents, large waves, and strong winds; where the ocean swallows
ships and sailors go to a watery grave. Cape Horn is located at the
southernmost point of South America, where the Atlantic Ocean
meets the Pacific at the headland of the Tierra del Fuego Archipelago. It is where offshore winds and strong currents push toward
the shoreline, threatening to dash ships against the rocky outcrops.

By March 21, we were experiencing snow and sleet. I remember
the date because I was on deck looking over the side, mesmerized
by the wake we made as we sliced through the water. I was beginning to feel the chill and tightened my wrap around myself as I
did not wish to catch a fever. Suddenly, two penguins leapt out of
the water beside us and crisscrossed back and forth amongst the

waves as if playing a game of "Catch Me If You Can." They were quite odd-looking animals but displayed a great charm and made me laugh. Then a large bird sidled up to the gunwale and kept pace with us for some time. When it had finished looking us over, possibly wondering what we were, it slipped quietly by without so much as a flap of its wings.

As treacherous as the ocean can be, it is also enticing in its power and beauty. The sea is capricious and uninhibited in temperament, yet it's unbound vastness and majesty holds you in its thrall. In so doing, it offers a sense of freedom and possibility to those who care to listen, but it is the master and you must obey its rules and understand its whims to survive.

As we approached the Cape, the wind freshened, and the waves became more chaotic. We stayed well south of the headland to avoid being blown against the lee shore. Once into the Pacific, we sailed north until we picked up the southeast trade winds, and then at around 5°S, we entered the doldrums—the sailor's nemesis where not a breath of wind can be found to fill the sails. Here, time seems to stop, and days of flagging listless sails can drive its captors to insanity. We were becalmed for weeks, but this gave us time to swab the decks, attend to the sails, check the rigging, and make repairs. Captain Barkley ran a clean ship, which was important for maintaining our health. Life took on a slow tempo. We were all more relaxed even though everyone was busy. I particularly loved our quiet evenings when, in the soft glow of the lantern, my husband taught me navigation and how to decipher the weather and I, in turn, instructed him in French.[1] We were both willing students and spent many enjoyable evenings engaged in such pursuits.

4

Impressions of Owyhee

THE FASTEST WAY to get to the Pacific Northwest was to sail west of our current position so that we could catch the northeast trades to Owyhee, after which we would sail farther north in a loop until we caught favourable winds to take us to King George's Sound (Nootka Sound). It had been a little over three months since we last saw land, but as the weather warmed, our spirits rose. Sea turtles and schools of fish started showing up in the waters around us, letting us know we were close to land. We spotted Owyhee on May 19. The air sweetened and the ocean took on a bluish-green colour that shimmered in the sunlight. As we drew closer to land, we noticed a large group of palms trees with their beautiful, variegated fronds gracing the shoreline. They were backed by deeply cut valleys that were rich in varying shades of green. We were some ways out from shore, about five or six leagues, when a great assembly of canoes paddled out to meet us.[1] A few of the paddlers came aboard and the canoes followed as we sailed closer in to set the anchor. Some of the women swam out to meet us and I marvelled at their dexterity in swimming, which was quite equal to the men. The women were very bold and forward and had no pretentions to beauty. They appeared to be quite healthy—none had leprosy that I could see—although both the men and women had sore eyes that were red and swollen, which might have been owing to the tropical sun and sea. From their curiosity, I surmised that before our arrival they had little contact with ships such as ours. After Captain Cook was killed here eight years before we arrived, no one had sailed to Owyhee, but with the beginning of the fur trade, it became an important stopover to replenish supplies before heading to King George's Sound.

Captain Barkley first dropped anchor off the largest of the islands. We were wary at first, but my husband was an honourable man and treated the Indigenous people we met (the Kānaka) with ceremony and respect. Still, we did not let our guard down. Trading was successful and, for us, very cheap. We were brought canoes full of fish, potatoes, taro, plantains, and hogs; in trade, the Kānaka were keen to have iron nails, tools, and any other bits of iron that we had.[2] One nail would gain us the most delicious pork that would feed the ship's crew for the day.

This was my first encounter with people who did not have their own supply of iron. When I think back, I realize they had been isolated until Captain Cook first sailed to Owyhee in 1778 and there would be no way for them to obtain iron except through trade. Years later, when we came back, I saw they had cleverly turned the nails into fishhooks, which were strong, unlike the ones made of fishbones, which were more fragile. They had also crafted knives and many other useful implements out of the iron.[3] One Kanaka who came on board was a man who was called Kamehameha. He was stately in comportment and much taller than any of us. He had the physique of powerful man. He seemed to be a chief as others paid him deference. He wore a cape about his shoulders that was made from bark cloth and festooned with thousands of brightly coloured yellow feathers. Despite his fierceness, he was very likable. We found him to be perceptive and shrewd, but also hospitable and kind. In respect of his status, we presented him with a pair of prize turkeys. He had never seen such a bird before and was pleased with the gift. Kamehameha exhibited a great deal of curiosity about us and our world. He was interested in trade and was particularly keen to obtain guns from us. After a few days of successful trading, we continued on sailing along the coast of Olowalu looking for a lee shore where it would be safe to drop the anchor.[4] Again, many canoes came out to great us and the shore was lined with people. It was an isolated location, and I don't think they had seen outsiders before. They looked us over with a great deal of curiosity and were especially intrigued with my red hair.

In one of the canoes, there was a young woman who came aboard. She spent some time looking around the ship and then indicated that she wished to stay with us. We could not understand their language, but its melodic overtones were soothing. The woman kept repeating the word Winée as she pointed to herself. I took that to be her name.[5] I welcomed the companionship and so we agreed to let her stay. I learned later that she was the first Kanaka woman to leave Owyhee to travel aboard a trading ship such as the *Imperial Eagle*. I cannot guess at her reason for staying aboard. Perhaps she yearned to reach beyond her shores.[6] She was, as I was, aboard a sailing ship for the first time, bound to places unknown by either of us. Winée would be my constant companion

Winée, 1794. PD-OLD-100

until we reached Canton, but more on that later. When we had replaced our water and food, the command was given to set sail on the long passage to the lands of the sea otter.

5

Nootka Sound, Fuca's Strait, and Tragedy

ON THIS LEG of our journey, we sailed over 2,500 nautical miles, heading first north and then east before reaching our destination.[1] The trip was long and the days began to merge together; there was no Monday or Tuesday or Wednesday. Our lives were ruled instead by wind, weather, trimming sails, noting the position of celestial bodies and the altitude of the sun, and working out complex mathematical calculations to approximate our location. Captain Barkley was a skilled navigator and had purchased the very best navigation equipment available. He had the latest marine chronometer, which was quite expensive. I still have his chronometer and will bequeath it to my grandson, John Trevor Barkley, with the understanding that it be preserved and passed on to his descendants. His sextant was a beautiful instrument. He used to it calculate our position of latitude by measuring the angle between a heavenly body and the horizon. Everyone aboard worked hard, there was little leisure time. The crew ate when they were off watch and slept when they

A View of the Habitations in Nootka Sound, circa 1770–1800.

could. They needed their rest, particularly as the weather could suddenly demand everyone be on deck to harness the wind.

As we reached the North Pacific High, the days lengthened and the winds dropped to a light breeze. At times, the ocean looked like a painting, smooth and glassy. I never tired of being out of sight of land, for the endless expanse of the ocean offered up mystery and an eclectic bounty of riches. There was always sea life around us. Sometimes we were accompanied by graceful albatross that hovered above us for hours on end. At other times pods of dolphins would play in our bow wave, and occasionally one of the large behemoths of the sea, a grampus,[2] would surface and spew its odoriferous breath high into the air, then swim in and out of the swells a few times before flipping its flukes at us then disappearing into the ocean depths. I observed things that I did not know existed. The strangest of all was a peculiar phenomenon we saw on our way to the Pacific Northwest. All around us the sea appeared to be covered with thousands of floating lights shimmering on the surface. It was captivating to watch, but the magic of these lights was lost when we saw them up close. The fairy-like iridescent glow that enthralled us was replaced by what looked like disgusting clusters of globs of fat. These clear-coated, blue underbelly creatures, I learned, are called Portuguese Man O' War. An apt name, as the long thread-like tentacles that stretch out behind them can be lethal if you touch them.

We approached King George's Sound in the month of June in 1787. We were a little worse for wear and very tired when we entered the sound as we had encountered another dreadful storm that hit us from the southeast. When we arrived, we found there were no other vessels in the sound, and apparently none in the immediate vicinity. Consequently, Captain Barkley did extremely well with his trade and soon procured all the furs the people had for sale. We were at the outer reaches of the trading empires and, like at Owyhee, I was the first European woman that had visited these shores. The *Imperial Eagle* was also the largest ship that had entered these waters. The climate here felt familiar as it was about the same as in Scotland, with perhaps a little more rain. However, the fruit ripened at a much more advanced season than the same berries did in England, or even in Scotland.

After we set the anchor in Friendly Cove, a canoe came alongside paddled by a man that was clothed in a greasy sea otter skin; he was disgustingly dirty. When he came aboard, to our astonishment he introduced himself as Dr. John MacKay. He then proceeded to tell us his story, which I will relay as it was extraordinary. He had been the ship's surgeon aboard the trading snow, the *Experiment*, under the command of Captain Henry Guise, when they entered King George's Sound the previous year together with the *Captain Cook*, commanded by Henry Laurie. He was suffering from scurvy at the time and was extremely ill and too weak to continue, so requested that he be left on shore in order to recover. Over the ensuing twelve months, he gradually improved and, while doing so, immersed himself in learning the language and ways of the people here. He had been well treated by Maquinna,[3] but after breaking a taboo, he was exiled from the community and sent to survive on his own, which is when he came to us. Captain Barkley engaged Dr. MacKay as a trader, a position that he carried out entirely to my husband's satisfaction. The knowledge Dr. MacKay gained over the many months spent in Friendly Cove helped Captain Barkley understand trading protocols. He also showed us the best places to obtain sea otter furs and we were able to eventually acquire seven hundred pelts and several lesser furs.

I was very impressed with Chief Maquinna and his bother Chief Callicum. These men were intelligent, active, and enterprising. We found Maquinna a skilled manager of the fur trade. We had heard that the people of this coast were shrewd traders and knew the value of their furs.

We were not long at Nootka when two ships, the 171-ton *Prince of Wales* and the 65-ton sloop *Princess Royal* entered the sound. Their many months of sea had taken its toll on both ships' crews. They were in poor condition and their supplies had run low. Their diet left them wanting and scurvy blighted the crew, leaving few healthy enough to manage. Captain Barkley provided them with paint oil and some black varnish along with a quarter cask of wine, hogshead (ale), and twenty gallons of brandy. They were prepared to pay for the liquor, but Captain Barkley politely returned the bill, desiring that it be left until we met in China. The rapport between the two men was respectful, but Captain James Colnett, the commander of the *Prince of Wales*, seemed aloof. He kept referring to our ship as the *Loudoun*, which it was when Captain Barkley let slip the lines at Shadwell Dock on September 7, 1786, for its maiden voyage to Ostend. But the name was changed to the *Imperial Eagle* while in Ostend.

Perhaps this is the time to explain how the *Imperial Eagle* came to be sailing under the Austrian flag. John Reid, the Austrian Consul in Canton, and Daniel Beale, the Prussian Consul in Canton, persuaded my husband to join their company and sail under the Austrian flag.

Over time, I learned that two companies, the East India Company and the South Sea Company, had a monopoly over maritime trade and any who were not in the employ of the EIC or were caught trading without the required permissions were subject to heavy fines and the offending ship confiscated. The East India Company controlled maritime trade east of Cape of Good Hope, and the South Sea Company from Cape Horn, along the west coast of the Americas to the Arctic, and 782 nautical miles into the Pacific. The required fees were extortionist, and while we would be allowed to sell our furs in Canton, the return trip to London would have to be in ballast. It would be impossible to make a profit. Many sea traders were angry over this monopoly and bypassed the East India and South Sea Companies by sailing under a foreign flag.[4] We were no different.

Captain Colnett had been with the British Royal Navy and had sailed with Captain Cook. He wrote a letter to Captain Barkley requesting that he show his authority for trading in the South Sea Company's territory. Captain Barkley hesitated, but eventually sent the papers of authorization. Captain Colnett still seemed uneasy but said nothing more to my husband; the papers were in German and perhaps he could not read them. Because of Captain Barkley's generosity toward the *Prince of Wales* and the *Princess Royal,* Captain Colnett wrote again to my husband saying that "Captain Berkley's behavior was as humane & Generous as I ever met with, and I am sorry his Busyness so clash'd with mine that I was oblig'd to behave in the distant manner I did."[5]

On July 24, we left Friendly Cove and turned southward. At 49°20'N, we came upon a large ocean inlet that Captain Barkley named Wickaninnish's Sound, the name given it being that of a chief who seemed to be quite as powerful a potentate as Maquinna at King George's Sound. Chief Wickaninnish had great authority and this part of the coast proved a rich harvest of furs for us. We sailed southward of this sound and came to another very large sound to which Captain Barkley gave his own name, calling it Barkley Sound. Several coves and bays and islands in this sound we named. There was Frances Island, after me, Hornby Peak, Trevor Channel, Cape Beale after our purser, Williams Point, and a variety of other names, all of which were familiar to us. We anchored in a snug harbour near the island, of which my husband made a chart as far as his knowledge of it would permit. The anchorage was close to a large village. We referred to the island as Village Island. By the morning of August 11, we were off the mouth of this sound, which appeared extensive, but of no great depth. Several islands were placed nearly in the middle of it, which were rather high, and well wooded. The longboat was sent to find the anchoring ground, and a little after 11:00 it returned to pilot us into a fine spacious port formed by several islands. We anchored in eight fathoms water over a muddy bottom, which made for a good hold. It was securely sheltered from wind and sea. Many people

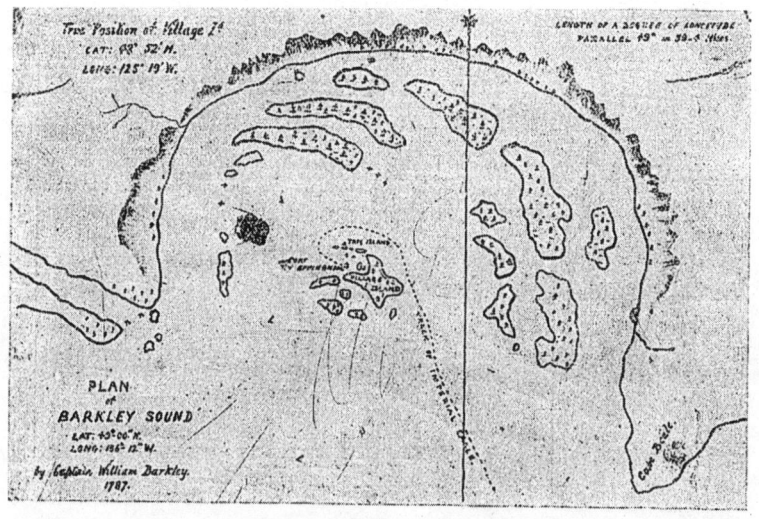

Plan of Barkley Sound, 1787, by Captain Charles Barkley.
COURTESY VICTORIA *TIMES COLONIST*, PUBLISHED ON MARCH 2, 1901

immediately came off in their canoes and brought an abundance
of fish, among which were salmon, trout, cray, and other shellfish,
with plenty of wild berries and onions. These people lived in a
large village situated on the summit of a very high hill. This port
we named Port Effingham in honour of the noble Lord of that title.

From Barkley Sound we proceeded eastward, and to the great
astonishment of Captain Barkley and his officers, a large opening
presented itself, extending miles to the east with no land in sight
in that direction. The entrance appeared to be about four leagues
in width and remained about that width as far as the eye could
see. Captain Barkley at once recognized it as the long-lost strait
of Juan de Fuca, which Captain Cook had so emphatically stated
did not exist.

We did not explore the strait, but instead continued along the coast. Our ship's position was 47°43'N when we anchored between a small island and the main shore. The coast appeared to be inhabited and two boats were sent up the river hoping to trade. Finding the water too shallow even for the longboat, it was decided that the smaller boat would be better able to navigate the river. Mr. Miller, Mr. Beale, and four seamen continued upstream, taking a sheet of copper with them to trade for furs. They were never seen again. The next day Captain Barkley mounted an armed party to go in search. They did not find the missing men nor the boat, but to their horror they did find portions of their clothes, which were torn and bloody. We had to assume they were murdered. My husband named the river Destruction River.[6] We later learned that Captain Meares, sailing in the *Iphigenia,* while anchored in Friendly Cove the following year, was offered for sale a withered hand and the ear of a person that had a seal earring attached. Mr. Miller always wore a seal earring. The person that approached Captain Meares disclosed that he had acquired the grisly items in trade.

After the incident, we were shocked and deeply saddened and decided to leave these shores immediately; it was now August. We turned northwest and sailed for Canton, arriving in Macao in November 1787. I did not record the trip across the Pacific in my notes and I am afraid my memory eludes me about this part of the journey.

6

The Hongs
of Canton

WE DROPPED ANCHOR at the port of Macao, a Portuguese enclave situated on a small peninsula bordered by the most beautiful bay that was filled with ships from many nations. Winée and I took up residence in a house made available to us by Mr. Cummings, one of the supercargoes, while my husband was taken up the Pearl River to Canton to trade our furs. Foreign women were not allowed beyond the city, so we settled into our lodgings.[1] Our house was quite elegant and had the most beautiful garden attached to it. I was told it was where Camoens, the famous seventeenth-century Portuguese poet who wrote *The Lusiads*, which I loved reading. The cave with the poet's seat was well preserved. It was an enchanting spot.

In the interim, First Officer Folger had a disagreement with Captain Barkley and left the *Imperial Eagle* in a fit of temper. We heard that he stayed in Macao until he found passage with Captain George Dixon on the *Queen Charlotte*. In the meantime, Captain Barkley, under the direction of a pilot, took the *Imperial Eagle* forty miles up the Bocca Tigris to the Pearl River and then

Hongs at Canton, circa 1820. PD-OLD-70

another farther ten miles to the Whampoa anchorage. He then had to wait for a sampan to ferry the cargo another fourteen miles up the river to Canton. Trading was very efficient. Each country was assigned to a specific Hong, or factory, for trade. The harbour was filled with sampans coming and going in a seemingly muddled tangle. Along a slip of land abutting the walled city of Canton were the thirteen Hongs, each with their identifying flags signaling a specific county. Our furs were offloaded at the Austrian factory, which was tucked behind the American garden and next to the Swedish factory. Trading was highly regulated, and fees were charged for everything; there was a fee for the pilot, another for a language translator, yet another for the agent, and one more for the dockhands. There was a weighing fee, rent for storage in the factory, a surtax, as well as import–export duties. Although the Chinese had little care for the foreign traders and viewed us with disdain, they did like the luxurious sea otter pelts we brought and gave a good price for them. Despite arriving early from Nootka, Captain Barkley was surprised to find the market flooded with furs from Russia. We were in the vanguard of the fur trade from Nootka and our furs were of the very finest quality. Their lustre, density, and softness made the red-rusty brown pelts utterly irresistible. It took a great deal of bargaining on my husband's part, but he procured £10,000 from the trading. We were delighted and the news of our good fortune quickly spread throughout the merchant service. This, unfortunately, was to be our undoing. I was beginning to learn that success sometimes breeds contempt and jealousy, which can bring out the worst in people, particularly those who wish to do you harm.

While Captain Barkley was in Canton, Winée and I were enjoying the pleasant weather of Macao. It was refreshing to be in such a temperate climate. I hoped the warmth might be of benefit to poor Winée as she was feeling quite ill, the cause of which I did not know. The city was a delight. Forts and churches situated atop the mountains enriched the scenery with their beautiful architecture and exotic gardens, and the streets below were enveloped in a fascinating maze of narrow, irregularly shaped passageways. It would be all too easy to get lost if it were not for the fact that we were ferried about in sedan chairs. It was a most European city.[2] There were balls, parties, teas, and dinners to attend. All of this was a bit startling, as I had become used to the quiet of the sea. Our first few days on land in cities were always a bit unnerving.

We weren't accustomed to the noise or the busyness of everyday life. Even walking on a flat surface that was not in constant motion was a bit destabilizing.

As the days wore on, Winée became weaker and was not able to do much more than rest. I enjoyed her company and although I had hoped to bring her to Europe, she said that she wanted to go home. As we were sailing in the opposite direction, passage would have to be procured with another ship. When it was time for us to set sail, we left her in Macao and only heard later of her fate. The *Felice*, commanded by Captain John Smith, was sailing to Owyhee, so he took her aboard. I understand they left Macao on January 22, 1788. It was fortunate for Winée that another from Owyhee was on board. His name was Kaiana and he was a Chief of great nobility and standing.[3] Kaiana and Winée became quite close during her brief time aboard. I hope he was able to bring comfort to her in her final hours, particularly as she was so far away from her home and family.[4] As the situation with Winée became more serious, Kaiana was said to have barely left her side, tending to her even at the expense of his own health. Despite his attentions, Winée grew weaker. She died fifteen days into her trip. Her body was commanded to the sea near the Island of Panay, in the Visayan group of the Philippines. Kaiana was bereft over the loss and mourned her deeply, wailing for days as was the custom in his homeland. Winée had acquired a few items on her trip that she held dear. Nearing her death, she gave Kaiana a plate-shaped looking glass, a bottle and basin made of the very finest China, and for his wife, a gown, hoop and petticoat, and a cap. She requested that all of the other items she had be given to her mother and father.

7

Birth and Betrayal
in Mauritius

SAILING ACROSS THE Indian Ocean is always a challenge. To avoid the cyclone season, it is best to leave around the end of December or early January. We left Macao and arrived at Port Louis in Mauritius in February 1788. Mauritius is off the eastern coast of Africa and about 500 nautical miles from Madagascar. It was an important repositioning point for ships sailing between Asia and Europe as the harbour was a haven from the cyclones that raged across these waters from November to April. I was looking forward to our stay as it was a French colony and I would be able find others to speak with in French. I love coming into a harbour because the whole of the shoreline offers up a visual perspective that is not obvious from shore. I found the port every bit as attractive as it was reported to be, a jewel in the middle of the Indian Ocean. The harbour itself was dominated by a semicircle of mountains, with Pieter Both standing out among them. About a third way from its crown, a luxuriant jungle opened and flowed down

down to the coastal plain until it reached a line of graceful palms whose bent shape paid homage to the brilliance of the cerulean-tinted sea. It was opulent in its fertility.

We were invited to stay with Monsieur and Madam Collignia, who were good friends of ours. It was a wonderful time for us. The town was filled with scientists, artists, French travellers, and officers and crew from visiting ships. There was much gaiety with dances, dinner parties, and ongoing festivities. At the time, I was with child. Captain Barkley continued to Calcutta to attend business while I stayed in Mauritius.[1] The birth of my twins was exceedingly difficult; I was in great distress and had only a local woman to help me.[2] Sadly, one of the twins did not survive. I did not know the pain of loss could be so cruel. I was bereft of any energy and had to dig deep within myself to find the strength I needed to tend to the needs of our dear little baby. We named our precious child William Hippolyte Andrew Barkley. Hippolyte was in honour of the Collignias for their kindness toward us; William and Andrew were the names of his great uncles.

While we were in Mauritius, a great injustice toward my husband was unfolding in India. In the end, he would be deprived of the *Imperial Eagle*, lose his commission, the ship's cargo, and supplies that were laid in for a ten-year trip, along with his navigation instruments, which were of the best quality and most expensive. His logs, charts, and payment due to him were also confiscated.

The facts are these. Captain Barkley was appointed to the command of the *Loudoun*, since named the *Imperial Eagle*, and was engaged to perform three voyages from the East Indies to Japan, Kamskatcha, and the unknown coast of North America, for which he was to have the sum of £3,000. The owners were supercargoes in China in the service of the British East India Company. On my

John Meares, 1790. PD-OLD-100

husband's arrival in China, the owners found the *Imperial Eagle* was not warranted for trade with China as the company was working privately, even if under the Austrian flag. Fearful of losing their own situations, the owners were obliged to sell the *Imperial Eagle* to avoid worse consequences. They wanted to extricate themselves from their bargain with my husband, who, having made provision according to the original contract made in London, would have been a loser to the sum of thousands of pounds. It was particularly galling as he made upwards of £10,000 for the owners. When

41

Captain Barkley arrived in Calcutta, he was relieved of his command and the two remaining trips were cancelled.

Captain Barkley brought an action for damages. The affair was arbitrated by merchants and my husband was awarded £5000, but he had no recourse to get back his property. The company falsely claimed that Captain Barkley was bound by contract to furnish the nautical instruments and personal stores. Later we found that Captain Meares, who had a seedy reputation at best, was secretly in the same employ as my husband, and worked it so that he was the one to gain all my husband's effects, despite the fact that he was trading illegally for furs. To make matters worse, Captain Meares then published Captain Barkley's discoveries claiming merit and, with the greatest effrontery, vilified my husband in the process. I have thought of Captain Meares many times over the ensuring years and have found he had no recourse to treat us so. Perhaps he wished to curry favour with the supercargoes of the *Imperial Eagle,* or maybe it was in his nature to be so duplicitous. We also learned that he had a reputation for having a wanton disregard of the truth. Chief Maquinna called him "Aita-aita Meares"—the lying Meares. Captain Dixon of the *King George* and *Queen Charlotte* said Captain Meares pandered in palpable falsehoods and misrepresentations, and Robert Haswell of the *Lady Washington* stated that Captain Meares would not hesitate to forfeit his word and honour. Though many years have passed, I have never been able to put this injustice and betrayal to rest in my mind.

8

Shipwrecked off
the Bay of Le Havre

FATE WAS NOT done with us yet. In 1789, we left Mauritius with
our dear little William to take passage to England with a Captain
Babcock, who bore a brutal character. We sailed around the Cape
of Good Hope, up the coast of Africa, passed around Spain, and
as we were nearing the northwestern coast of Normandy, owing to
the bad management of the captain, we hit a sandbank. We were
wrecked off the Banque de I'Edain in the Bay of Le Havre. While
there are sandbars near this coastline, a competent navigator would
have had little difficulty avoiding them. Captain Barkley, myself
and our infant son, a pupil of my husband's, and two faithful fol-
lowers found ourselves alone on the wreck the morning after she
struck, the vile captain and his crew having deserted us and the
ship in the night. The ship's bottom was beaten in, but the cargo,
being cotton, kept it afloat. With the assistance of every boat in
the harbour, the ship was towed into Harfleur, where she foun-
dered and was lost. After a few days trying to sort ourselves out, we
took passage on one of the regularly scheduled packet ships that

ran between Portsmouth and Harfleur. When we entered the narrow entrance to Portsmouth Harbour and passed by the landmark Round Tower, we were greatly relieved. All the trials that beset us were momentarily pushed into the back of our thoughts as we rejoiced in the familiarity of our surroundings. We were just twelve days short of three years at sea, having left Ostend on November 24, 1786, and arriving in Portsmouth on November 13, 1789.

We settled in for a restful time ashore. I shall not bore you with an inventory of our daily life. Suffice it to say, to be able to visit with family and old friends and partake in meals that were not primarily made up of salt pork and rice was a joy. Daily tasks and taking care of little William were fraught with much less difficulty than when aboard ship. Life took on a predictable routine, although my husband was greatly occupied with organizing the direction of our next undertaking.

After spending seven months in England, we decided that we would return to India to settle and Captain Barkley, being eminently qualified, would engage in the country trade from port to port there. To risk another loss in the long-distance maritime trade, he reasoned, would be foolhardy. Captain Barkley had grown up in Calcutta and was well versed in the country's commerce. He believed Calcutta would afford us a comfortable life. He had family there and was a favourite of his great aunt Mrs. Ann Barkley-Forbes and her husband. Mr. Forbes was a successful merchant in Calcutta and would be a great support in our new venture. Calcutta was the centre of the country trade and a British East India Company town. My husband, having been in their employ, thought it would put him in good stead. We enjoyed the challenges ahead, and the gaiety of the balls and parties, and felt the life would suit us. This would be a good move for our family.

9

Summer in Copenhagen

AS A START for our new venture, Captain Barkley took command of the 1,200-ton merchant vessel, the *Princess Frederica*, of which he held a part share. The ship was bound for India but lay alongside the quay at Elsinore in Copenhagen. We gathered what we needed and the three of us made our way there from England. The *Princess Frederica* was a grand ship, built of the finest India teak. It would take our family in comfort to our destination. When we arrived, the ship was not yet ready for departure. There seemed to be endless delays. As my sister was living in Copenhagen with her husband, the temporary adjournment provided the opportunity to spend the summer months visiting. But when the long warm days slowly shifted into fall and the North Sea winds beckoned, we neared the date of our departure. Loaded with 1,500 bars of iron, liquor, and a few other articles for trade in Bombay, the *Princess Frederica* was ready. We boarded our passengers and said our goodbyes to friends and family, and on October 8, 1790, we let slip our mooring lines.[1] Keeping Kronborg Castle to port, formidably dignified in its stature, we rounded the tip of the peninsula and our sails filled as we met the North Sea. The concerns and worries one encounters on land were temporarily put aside as we turned our attention to matters at hand. A familiar rhythm asserted itself and life once again was taken over by the whims of powers greater than we.

10

Birth in a Storm

OUR ROUTE WOULD take us first south through the English Channel, down the west coast of Africa, around the Cape of Good Hope, stopping at Mauritius, and from there north to Bombay. Like Cape Horn, the Cape of Good Hope had a reputation of being a difficult expanse of water to transit, but by now I had weathered many storms and, while each was unique, I knew what to expect. No longer was I that young, inexperienced girl that left Ostend several years before. What I did not know was that when we left Copenhagen, I was with child. By the time we reached the Cape of Good Hope, I was nearing the end of my term and realized it would not be long before we welcomed a new member to our family. A baby's timing for birth gives no care to worldly happenings. Martha, whom we called Patty, decided to make herself known to the world just as we were rounding the Cape in a violent gale. Captain Barkley was fighting to keep the ship stable, maneuvering through the confused seas and steep waves, each in a hurry to overtake the other. All the while, I was being buffeted about and struggling with labour pains. I could feel the ship lurching from wave to wave and hear the wind screaming through the rigging. Bracing against

East Indiaman, Cape of Good Hope, 1786, by Robert Dodd. PD-OLD-100

the ship's movement made the whole process even more trying. Memories of my last experience giving birth flooded my thoughts, but irrespective of the violence of the moment, our dear Patty was born and open to the wonderous adventures that life had to offer. Soon after we rounded the Cape of Good Hope, the ship settled, and we welcomed the light airs and fair weather.

11

Food Shortages and Mauritius

WE WERE A month away from Mauritius and were running low on our food supplies as the weather at the Cape had delayed our arrival. On Sunday, May 29, we served out the last of the ship's bread that was still edible. I would never again take the smell of baking bread for granted. Fortunately, on June 4, we spied the tall mountains that marked Port Louis and were thankful we would soon be in port. Even though our visit would be just long enough to replenish our supplies, we were looking forward to the rest. We moved ashore for the week while the ship was being readied for the next leg of our journey. The ship's crew got to work immediately and by the fourth day in port Captain Barkley had the guns mounted for our journey north. The Malabar coast is an area where pirates lay in wait to raid vessels such as ours. They went after the bigger ships because the bulky East Indiamen were slow and could easily be overtaken. For that reason, ships usually travelled in convoys for safety. We were in the middle of monsoon season, though, and due to the likelihood of both ship and cargo being damaged, shipping along the coast ceased until after September. We would be on our own, bad weather and our guns offering up the only deterrence. We stored ninety fowl of various sorts, six hogs, four goats, plantains, potatoes, squashes, sweet potatoes, corn, and onions, twenty-one cases of wine, and water. Three of the crewmen mutinied and were sent to confinement aboard the frigate *Medusa*, to be discharged later. On June 12, we weighed the bower anchors and set the sails, anxious to get on our way. We were already behind schedule, but due to light winds were not able to depart for four more days. As was custom, we saluted the commodore with nine guns as we left the harbour.

12

Raging
Monsoons

WE HOPED TO be able to get to Bombay before we were hit with the full force of the southwest monsoons. We had been at sea for twenty-one days when, early in the evening of July 5, the weather became eerily calm. The sea was luminous and we could see the shadow of our ship glide against the waves. The barometer suddenly fell an inch, and not long after, the winds increased and became erratic. Then the rain, such as I had never seen, came pelting down. It was impossible to see anything. The rain was so thick that it created an impenetrable barrier between our ship and the land. We were sailing blind, which put us in a precarious situation. We had no option but to stand out (stay offshore). The next day the weather had cleared long enough to catch a glimpse of Malabar Point and the lighthouse on Old Woman's Island, which signalled the entrance to the harbour.[1] But the wind and rain came on again and the seas were immeasurably high. Try as we might, there was no hope of standing to the north. We were so close to our destination, but owing the wind and the tempestuous seas,

Captain Barkley decided it would be folly if we persisted. If a gale of wind came on, we might be dashed against the coast. Our provisions were down, so it was decided to try and find a port eastward. Once we were away from the Malabar coast and into the Bay of Bengal, the sea state calmed somewhat, although we still were contending with moderate gales. We had been at sea for thirty-nine days when, on July 23, we were finally in sight of Madras. We anchored in nine fathoms for the night, taking a berth the following the day. After all that we had endured, our passengers couldn't wait to put their feet on solid land. They gladly went ashore while Captain Barkley took care of the ship's business and brought in fresh provisions. Very early in the morning of August 15, at 3:00 AM, we slipped our lines and came to sail. We stood out for about five hours waiting for favourable winds, then we turned northward to sail toward the top end of the Bay of Bengal and the entrance of the Hooghly River. When we reached the river, we picked up a pilot who took us the eighty miles to our destination. Along the way, we were nearly swamped by the tide in the river. Finally, on August 22, we secured the *Princess Frederica* alongside the docks in Calcutta. This was going to be our home.

13

Calcutta

UNTIL WE FOUND a place of our own, we stayed in comfort with Captain Barkley's aunt and uncle, Mr. and Mrs. Forbes (neé Ann Barkley). One of the first things we did was to have Patty baptized. We asked them to be our dear child's godparents and were delighted when they accepted. We soon found a handsome house and furnished it with some of the items we brought with us. Buying furniture in Calcutta was a difficult task, for despite the vast movement of East Indiamen in and out of the harbour, furniture was not often brought in and when it was, it was quite costly. In all other respects, Calcutta was a thriving city, and, despite the unrelenting heat, life was full. There were dinner parties during the week and candle-lit formal balls on Fridays, although sometimes it was simply too hot to dance. On Sundays, there was church to attend, but for some it was less about maintaining their souls and instead served as a meeting place for single men to meet young women, particularly when a ship arrived bringing British girls of marriageable age. Card games were a popular pastime, whist was a favourite, and everyone was devoted to reading the gossip written up in the *Bengal Gazette*. When the smokiness of the city became

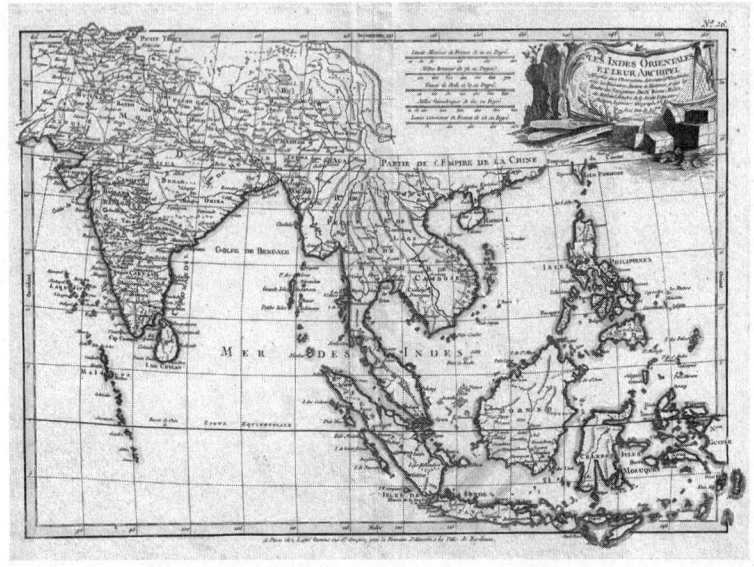

Map of India, Southeast Asia, the East
Indies, 1770, by Robert Bonne. PD-OLD-100

too much, we all strolled along the waterfront, where the light breezes cooled and sweetened the air. For many of the women, life in Calcutta was wrapped in indulgent idleness, particularly in the summer months when the intensity of the heat accompanied by the cloying stickiness in the air affected even the most enterprising. Ill health was common and the best escape was sleep. As I was new to Calcutta, I had much to learn and was too busy settling into our life and caring for our children to be so outwardly affected.

It was good to put down roots and move into a home after years at sea, and far easier for the children as well. We had made the right decision and were enjoying our time. That was, until that fateful day when our evil star brought my husband's older brother,

Captain John Barkley, into port. He was a British East India Company captain and in command of the 800-ton East Indiaman, *Lord Hawkesbury*. It was a ship he had been master of for the last three years. He was on his second voyage and came to visit after unloading his cargo in Bombay. As a captain in the employ of the EIC, he was vehemently opposed to my husband becoming a country captain, asserting that it was beneath his standing. He professed that he would not see his brother demean himself in an occupation that was held in such low esteem. My husband had been fretting over the amount of time it was taking to establish himself, particularly as the markets were in a temporary slump. He began to despair of selling his cargo and was alarmed at the expense of establishing such a business, even though fortunes were to be had in the country trade. In the 1790s, there were fifteen agency houses in Calcutta and increasing quickly. Captain Barkley was not a patient man, and it was relatively easy for his older brother to convince him to give up his plan.

From this time on, all our misfortunes took their rise, and are all attributable to the advice and fatal influence of Captain John Barkley. At the urging of his brother and blinded by the spirit of enterprise, my dear husband was persuaded to partner with Mr. Anthony Lambert of Calcutta, a highly influential and successful merchant who had come to Calcutta as a cadet with the EIC in 1781. Seeing a business opportunity in the country trade, the following year he left the employ of the EIC and established the merchant house of Lambert & Ross. They produced sugar, rum, and arrack of the finest quality. Trade with China was expanding, and Mr. Lambert knew of my husband's experience, and so befriended him. My husband was easily influenced by the sagacity of his new pretend friend to purchase two paltry vessels. They were bought at a great cost, with my husband providing one half of the funds and Mr. Lambert the other. Captain Barkley would command the 80-ton brig *Halcyon*, while the smaller 60-ton *Venus* was commanded by a great rascal. The *Halcyon* was to sail to Japan, the Kuril Islands, and Kamskatcha, trading for furs. Both ships were to eventually meet up at Nootka Sound.

There was discussion between my husband and his brother as to whether I should stay in Calcutta with the children. In fact, Captain John Barkley insisted upon it. He said his brother would be gone for less than twelve months and upon his return we would be set up financially and our family would want for nothing. There was pressure on me from all sides to stay with the Lambert family. I do admit their house was beautiful, situated as it was on the banks of the Hooghly. I was assured that the children and I would be afforded every luxury. I may have been young, but I was not naive. It was a credulous suggestion. No one saw the impropriety of the plan but me. I knew my husband did not really wish to be separated from me, nor I from him, for that matter. To relieve him from the burden of decision, I made plain my desire and firm determination to travel together. I told him that I would rather brave every danger than separate here, which was true. It seemed to appease him, but our hearts were heavy. Caught up in the journey, neither of us weighed the difference in comfort and safety between the *Halcyon* and the *Imperial Eagle*. Had we done so, we might have given it more thought.

PART II

VICTIMS OF OUR FOLLY

SECOND VOYAGE, DECEMBER 1791 TO DECEMBER 1794

14

The *Halcyon* and the Mighty Hooghly River

TO PROCEED, THEN. Our unpromising voyage began under every disadvantage. The *Halcyon* was completely unsuitable for our family and did not appear to be safe or steadfast for the conditions we would meet during such a long journey across open ocean. There would be little space for us on board, and small ships do not take as easily to the rigours of the ocean as do larger ones such as the *Imperial Eagle* or the *Princess Frederica*. Several people had mentioned such misgivings in their conversations with us. Although our brig was fast and manoeuvrable, it required a large crew to attend to the rigging, something we would have to forgo due to the increased cost. Adding to the precariousness of our situation, our crew were lascars, local sailors who were noted for their hard work but could not be depended on in a crisis. Moreover, most had never been so far away from their home port and would not be used to the conditions wrought by the sea. As for the timing of our trip, it was too late in the season to take advantage of the regular trade winds. Whatever our fate, I would bear what came with dignity and stand as a support to my husband.

We left Calcutta in late December 1791. We hired a pilot who took us down the Hooghly River to the entrance of the Bay of Bengal. The Hooghly was a long and winding river that was difficult and dangerous to navigate in places, with its shifting sands, large tidal bores, and fast currents. It could not be transited without the experienced guidance of a pilot. Even so, on our way up, we nearly breached. The river itself is impressive and its beauty helped us temporarily forget the ease and comfort we had left behind. As we moved farther down the river and the grand houses that lined the banks began to disappear, the land was taken over by the leafy splendor of the jungle and vast tracts of mangrove forests with their strange tangle of roots. It was here where tigers and other wild animals roamed freely. In the early evening, under the glow of the setting sun, reds, yellows, and oranges spatter the river with their mellow hues, but at night, when the riverbanks darken, the persistent, piercing howls of jackals were unnerving and frustrated our sleep. It is said their howling is a portent of misfortune and death.

On our seventh day on the river, we passed Diamond Harbour, the last port before the Bay of Bengal. We moored at Cox's Island, where we found the *Phoenix*, an East Indiaman bound for Calcutta. This was a bit of luck as Captain John Barkley was to have arranged a tender for us, which was a smaller boat that we would secure to the deck. Not only would it act as a safety vessel in case we had to abandon ship, but it would be used to ferry us to and from shore. It would be unwise to leave without it, for we did not have our full complement of boats. We were disappointed by the negligence of Captain John, who never forwarded any orders to the officer in change—very brotherly conduct! Not only did Captain Alexander Gray kindly take our pilot back up the Hooghly, but he was instrumental in procuring us a boat from one of the pilot schooners at this station. Noting the condition of our ship, Captain Gray said that taking a vessel such as the *Halcyon* deep sea seemed a most dangerous undertaking. But, he added, if talent, prudence, and good seamanship could guarantee success, Captain Barkley would ensure it.

15

Entrance to
the Spice Islands

ON JANUARY 7, Captain Barkley took control of the *Halcyon*, and we sailed out through the river delta with the *Venus*, turning our backs on all that could have been. Leaving Sagar Island to port, both ships carefully manoeuvred around the perilous sandbanks that stood as sentinels to the Bay of Bengal. The weather was fine and there was little motion. I was beginning to think that our small brig would not be such an inconvenience after all. During the night, though, I became dissuaded from that thought. As we approached the entrance to the Sunda Strait, a fierce wind arose, and the seas became boisterous. We were tossed around in all directions as if we were an insignificant scrap of wood. We were completely the sport of the waves. Several times we thought the *Venus* would be lost as we watched it slide down the face of a wave on its side, its keel exposed. The rain fell in torrents and the lascars who were driven below almost drowned. All ports and hatches were closed, and the children and I stayed below in the stifling heat. It was close, humid, and hard to breathe, besides which it

Map of the East Indies and Southeast Asia, 1801, by John Cary. PD-OLD-100

was impossible to maintain our footing. Once again, I was thankful that I did not experience seasickness as the malady renders one violently nauseous, powerless, unable to move, and diminishes any desire to survive. The poor dear children were suffocating and I thought they would be sick. The two girls we brought with us for help were terrified and very seasick, and so took to their berths. I had to manage the children on my own. We were ten days in that weather trying to sail through the entrance to the Sunda Strait.

Finally, on January 25, we had a fine breeze and fair weather and entered the strait, leaving the island of Java to starboard. We had now crossed into the exotic world of the East Indies and the famed Spice Islands, which were dotted with coral islets, sandy beaches, and coastal mangroves. The Sunda Strait was not the easiest channel to navigate. We had to contend with strong tidal currents, sandbanks, poor charting, reefs, and shallowing at its eastern end. On January 27, we set our anchor in a bay at

Kakatoire, a small island midway in the strait.[1] Kakatoire was rather peculiar. It was very steep and looked like a tall cone or hat, depending on what angle you looked at it. It was well covered with trees, many of them exceedingly large. There was a small village of about one hundred Malay living near a freshwater spring. Every day while we were at anchor, I would go ashore for a stroll and made sure I passed by the grove of mango trees that were heavy with ripe luscious fruit. Mangoes have a juicy, delectable sweetness to them that is irresistible. I was careful not to stray too far, remembering the experience of poor Mr. Beale near Nootka Sound. We took in wood, filled up our water casks, and brought on board turtles, plantains, mangoes, coconuts, and pumpkins, along with a variety of melons, all provided by the villagers. The evening before we were to leave, we experienced a dreadful thunderstorm. Lightning flashed all over, and one clap of thunder laid us prostrate on the deck. The *Halcyon* was untouched, but the *Venus* was not so favoured; lightning struck its mainmast and splintered it, together with the main topmast, foremast, and top gallant mast. After repairs, we departed on February 3. The next, day we stopped at Bantam on the northwest coast of Java, and on the following day, we picked our way through the many reefs that are scattered about the anchorage at Batavia Road. The only memory I have of Batavia was that it was hot and humid, and it was the centre of the Dutch East India Company's trade in Asia, much as Calcutta was for the British EIC.

I am less sure of the dates and the order of events for the next part of our journey as I have been unable to find any data to go by. However, a long train of misfortunes succeeded this part of the voyage.

16

Heartbreak in Celebes

FROM BATAVIA, WE turned north into the Java Sea and heart of the Spice Islands, where cinnamon, nutmeg, cloves, and mace were highly sought after. There was nowhere else in the world that could equal the beautiful scenery with its broad terraces of variegated greens and carpets of dense trees spilling down to the water's edge. The most luxurious perfume, warm and sultry, scented the air and followed us throughout all these islands. We were headed toward the Makassar Strait, and despite the distraction of this wonderous oasis, we needed to be on our guard—the strait was a well-known lair for pirates. With thousands of islands to hide in, they lay in wait in the coves and bays for a ship such as ours to sail by. We no longer had our cannons and size to protect us and were vulnerable. I was particularly concerned as we now had our two small children to consider. When we entered the strait, we were met with a strong current running against us and little wind to speak of. Consequently, we made barely any headway. For three weeks, our attempts to gain ground were thwarted. Some evenings, after a day of tacking back and forth, we found ourselves nearly in the same spot from whence we started. It was quite disheartening, but at least we were not going backwards. On one evening, our attention was mercifully diverted when we noticed a commotion near the hull. We were surprised to see small eddies swirling around us. Looking for the cause, we found a freshwater stream flowing out from the land, skimming the surface as it coursed over the denser ocean water. Immediately, all hands set to work filling up the casks. Even though the water was a little brackish, fresh water was always welcomed and we took what we could get. While not drinkable, there were many other uses to which it could be put. As our pace was set to the speed of a garden snail, we spent our time fishing and delighting in the scenery around us. The night sky was equally impressive as millions of stars, strewn across the celestial heavens, dazzled against the backdrop of the black void beyond. The very movement of the constellations laid out a map for us, which Captain Barkley used to determine our headings. As we were wrapped in this blanket of blissful delight, we were completely unaware of a great misfortune that was in store for us.

We had been working our way slowly up Makassar Strait when my beloved husband was attacked with a dreadful disease. He had a high fever and a violent colic. The pain was excruciating and it threw his body into such contortions that two men could hardly restrain him. He turned all colours and sometimes appeared as if he was dead. I never left his side. We did not carry a ship's doctor, so I ministered to him as best I could. I mixed a purgative from the medicines we had with us. He slowly recovered, but it left him dreadfully debilitated.[1] It was not long after that our dear little Patty began displaying the same symptoms. She was feverish, sweating, and listless. She kept pulling her knees up tight against her stomach, attempting to ease the terrible pain she was in. I held her in my arms trying to comfort her. I was beside myself, but I needed to remain calm. She looked drawn and so helpless that I knew we were losing her. She struggled valiantly, but her small body was not able to withstand the assault that had taken hold of her. Her breathing became weaker and less stable, and then she took one last breath and her body slackened. On April 15, just one day short of her first birthday, our dear babe died in my arms.[2] We were devastated. If we had not come on this doomed trip, my husband would not have been sick and our child would still be alive. Because of our folly, she did not get that chance. In her brief life, she had spent only four months ashore. She was a child born of the sea, but it was not where she would be laid to rest. A leaden box was prepared for her remains in order that they might be kept until we could reach the nearest port of call. It was important for us to bury our beautiful child in consecrated grounds, and consequently we sailed to Celebes, an island governed by the Dutch East India Company. The largest port was Makassar, at the southern end of Celebes. It was one of the most beautiful ports in the Spice Islands. We were not allowed to disembark as the Dutch East India Company jealously guarded inroads from other companies, particularly the EIC, a sworn enemy. From the ship, we could see a town stretch out before us with lovely gardens and neat rows of houses. We were met by the Dutch Resident and told him of our desire to bury our daughter in concentrated ground. He immediately refused and, worse yet, was indifferent to our plight. His intransigence made our feeling of loss so much more heartbreaking. As merchant traders we were used to bargaining, so after much negotiation it was agreed that Patty could be buried ashore, but we would not be allowed to pay our last duties to our dear child. We would have to be content to watch the ceremony from the ship. With heavy hearts, we lowered the tiny casket over the gunwale and onto a small boat. We stood in silence as our precious cargo moved farther and farther away from us, oar stroke by oar stroke, until we could see her no longer. The spot where she was deposited is one of the most beautiful in the world. She lies under the shade of a grove of coconut trees.

Captain Barkley then gave the order to weigh anchor, and with favourable winds, the crew hoisted the sails and the *Halcyon* and *Venus* turned northeast to continue our journey. That evening, my husband noted in his log, "Interred my Dear Child in the burying ground ashore." He wrote nothing in his log for the following five days, such was his sadness. Our grief was profound. After being buffeted about from island to island, we made our way through the Maluku Archipelago, the heart of the Spice Islands, sailing between Gelolo and Margion and then into the Pacific Ocean. The current was with us and we flew through this chain of islands at around ten to twelve knots. It was as if we were sailing on a beautiful river. Between two of the islands, the strait was so narrow that we might have spoken to the people on shore, had there been any. Despite the narrowness of the channel, the water was quite deep. Our lead line was run out to the ten-fathom line (eighteen metres) and still had not found the bottom. I shall never forget the beautiful scenery that these islands presented. They seemed like a fairy land, rising in green terraces, one above the other in the most graceful slopes, each covered with groves of elegant trees. The beaches were gleaming white and the water near the shore was translucent.

From there, we moved out into the Pacific, where we parted with the *Venus*. It was a fast-sailing cutter and would reach the

Pacific Northwest before we would. We bade them goodbye, and I silently wished them luck as Captain Shepherd was a great brute to his crew. We were once again in open ocean where our only marker was a thin line in the far distance that separated the deep blue of the sea from the paleness of the sky, creating a variegated illusion of oneness. The only way to know where we were under such conditions was to pay heed to our navigational instruments. Captain Barkley's charts were always open on his chart table and were covered with astronomical calculations.

CHAPTER

17

The Western Pacific and the Caroline Islands

IT WAS SOMETIME time in May—I am not certain of the date—
but we had been running downwind at a good speed, ten knots,
and were it not for daylight, we would have beached ourselves on
one of the New Carolina islands. The Spanish charts we had were
inaccurate and we arrived before expected. Had it been foggy or
a half hour later, which was when darkness set in, the *Halcyon*
would have been lost. It was a narrow escape. The island was gir-
dled by sunken rocks and coral reefs that would swiftly rip holes
into our hull.

Nine canoes came out to meet us. Looking toward the shore we
could see a great number of outriggers lined up along the beach.
The boats looked to be well made and were painted with stripes of
red and white. They were constructed from planks sewn together
and sat rather high out of the water. Each canoe was very narrow
and was pointed at both the bow and stern and was balanced by
a log that acted as an outrigger. The people appeared to have seen

ships such as ours before as they did not show any fear or astonishment. However, it was only when we lowered down a few spike nails that they came along side and made fast their canoes, and only one of the more than fifty men from the canoes came on board to trade. For iron nails they gave us some flying fish, which were good for bait, a few ornaments they wore in their ears, and coconuts. They appeared to be very healthy, but not quite so athletic as the Kānaka. They were large and well-proportioned with fine features and very bushy hair that hung loose about their shoulders. Their bodies were entirely tattooed in different patterns. They wore tortoise shell bracelets on their arms and a kind of coarse carnelian and coral-strung necklace around their necks. Their ears were perforated and appended with large shells, which had elongated the apertures. On their heads, they wore caps made of a type of matting in a tall, conical shape, much like that of a sugarloaf. They understood a few words that were spoken to them in the language of the Sandwich Islands peoples, whom they resembled in their manners and gestures. They told us the name of their island was Yap. The island was beautifully wooded and their houses, which we could only see through our telescope, had slanted roofs that looked like our European farmhouses. They appeared to be well built, the best we had seen in the South Seas. As we turned toward the sea, we were followed by several of the canoes. The *Halycon* was copper bottomed, which helped to protect the hull and keep us running through the water smoothly and swiftly. The paddlers matched our speed effortlessly, but soon departed. By the evening, we were becalmed. To our surprise, two canoes made an appearance, followed by several others, even though we stood out about three or four leagues (nine to twelve miles) from shore. Our visitors were villagers from the west end of Yap. Looking toward the shore, we could see a large village situated in a stand of coconut trees. It looked very green and pleasant to the eye. When the wind picked up, we turned north toward Japan.

18

South Island and Sulphur Island

ON JUNE 16, we came upon a dangerous rock called South Island. I referred to it as a rock because it hardly deserved the name of an island. It rose straight out of the ocean and was formed in the shape of a tall pinnacle, the top of which was lost in the clouds. We all agreed that it was volcanic.[1] Captain Barkley circumnavigated it in the longboat looking for a place to land, but its high bluffs and surging seas made that impossible. I mention this because its existence was in great doubt among nautical men. It had only been noted once before, and my husband's survey of the rock affirmed the findings of Captain John Gore, who was the first to come upon it. He sailed with the Royal Navy as well as with Captain Cook and had circumnavigated the globe four times. He was one of the most knowledgeable mariners of the Pacific. Unfortunately, he died just a year before we began this leg of our journey.

Captain Barkley was very desirous of making Sulphur Island, which was only about thirty-two nautical miles from South Island.

South Island and Sulphur Island

We were told of its wonderous sulphur beds. Sadly, we could not see the island as it was shrouded in dense fog when we passed by.

By now, we had sailed around 1,100 nautical miles since leaving the Caroline Islands. The Pacific Ocean is immense in its breadth and is sparsely populated. To see its name plated on a chart is one thing, but to experience such limitlessness is humbling. Day by day, we sailed farther north and east. To indicate where we were, Yap was 1,700 nautical miles northeast from Celebes (9°55'N, 135°13'E), the Sulphur Islands were in the Western Pacific, south of Japan (24°7'N, 141°31'E), and Paramocha, our next destination, was a farther 2,000 nautical miles into the North Pacific (50°23'N, 155°49'E).

19

Endless Fog and Rain in the North Pacific

AS WE MOVED farther north, our charts were noticeably more inaccurate. It certainly did not help that we were shrouded in dense fog, which appeared to be permanently affixed to the landscape. We weren't quite certain where we were as it had been impossible to take sights for days.[1] We did have a vague sense that we were somewhere near the Kurile Islands but did not want to transit the archipelago in such conditions. The whole of this forlorn locality was most dreary. The weather was cold and damp, choking out all our bodily warmth. That, and the constant drizzling of rain and mist that seeped into our clothing, made us feel miserable. The transition from the fine summer warmth we had enjoyed before to this dismal weather was trying. We found ourselves in a delicate situation with regards to our health. The poor lascars were accustomed to the warmer temperatures in India and found it impossible to adjust. Many became seriously ill, as did I. Up until this time, I had enjoyed good health, which gave me the courage

I needed to endure such dangers and to submit to privation. But in these climes, I shivered, my face swelled, and my teeth ached.

On June 16, we were overjoyed when we caught a glimpse of a snow-topped mountain. It stood out like an alluring jewel, but quickly vanished as the smoky grey clouds settled in again and the former dull scene was renewed. Land was spotted again the following day and we reckoned we were at the south end of the island of Paramocha, one of the northernmost islands close to the Kamchatka Peninsula. In all, it took us six months from leaving our home in Calcutta to reach these rich waters where the sea otter dwelled. The dull uniformity of our environment was suddenly enlivened by an announcement from the masthead—a Russian galliot had been sighted. Their astonishment at being hailed by a foreign vessel must have been great, but when they noticed our colours, they altered their course and ran before the wind, perhaps uncertain of our intent. However, the *Halcyon*, being a fast ship, quickly caught up to the galliot. After we came alongside and with promises of gifts, Captain Barkley went aboard the Russian ship, taking with him a cask of English porter and some madeira wine, for which they were quite thankful. He was able to confirm our location, which corresponded with his own reckoning. They had a few sables aboard that my husband purchased. He was also able to obtain several warm dog-skin greatcoats for the lascars, who were perishing with the cold. The captain's lady, who was a very handsome young woman, sent me a small sable muff and expressed her wish to come aboard and to meet an English woman. Regrettably, their captain, who was as uncouth as his ship, would not allow it. I was thankful for the gift. The sable was silky-smooth to the touch, although not quite as thick and rich as the fur otters. The Russian captain brought out a few more skins, for which he extracted an exorbitant price from our ship's stores. There were several ladies lined up along the deck of the galliot, passengers most likely. They looked to be Russian women, fair and attractive. It was a welcome sight. Not being able to visit on board, we gestured to each other, laughed, and nodded, none of us really understanding the other, but enjoying the contact nonetheless.

20

Parties in Petropavlovsk

WE CONTINUED TOWARD Petropavlovsk, which is on the south-east coast of the Kamchatka Peninsula. It was here that we hoped to obtain enough furs to make our long trip worthwhile. Along the way, we were teased with momentary glimpses of snow-capped mountains before the veil of fog enveloped us once again. We were aware of the long chain of mountains that lined this coast, but we lived within this bubble of featureless whiteness and could see nothing. According to Captain Barkley's calculations, we were nearing our destination. On June 21, and much to our favour, as we came abreast of the lighthouse signaling the entrance to Awat-cha Bay, our old nemesis the fog lifted. To our amazement, winter suddenly became summer; the cold north wind dropped and the warmth coming off the land was a welcomed surprise. We entered the bay with some trepidation as we had heard the Russians dis-liked foreign traders, particularly the British. They were fiercely protective of their furs. Unexpectedly, three great guns were fired. We could see soldiers, with their muskets shouldered, standing in

Petropavlovsk, Kamchatka, Mount Avatcha in
Background, n.d., by Thomas Know. PD-OLD-70

a cloud of white smoke near where the cannons were fired. They
were clad in thick bear skins, which made them look more like
the animals than men. On the opposite side, we noticed six more
cannons. There seemed to be more guns than men guarding the

entrance to the bay. After that rather unnerving welcoming, a boat was dispatched with a pilot aboard to show us where we should anchor. Once around the peninsula, the bay itself was expansive and was dominated by lofty snow-capped mountains that loomed over everything. It was quite magnificent. Mariners rightfully call this the "Kamchatka Pearl."

As soon as we anchored, the sergeant came aboard with greetings and a gift of two large salmon from the governor, Major Ismailov. The area was rich in fish, particularly salmon. We were assured that the fish had been carefully prepared according to custom and were buried for several days. The sergeant was eager to have us try this tasty morsel. I need not describe what we thought, but we suppressed our revulsion and in the name of diplomacy, we ate the rotting fish with good cheer. It was something I would not want to repeat. We were then offered an invitation to join the governor the following day, which we graciously accepted. We dressed the *Halcyon* in the appropriate flags, gathered our family together along with our ship's officers, and rowed to shore. We were greeted with great ceremony and a repast of salmon was specially prepared for us in the same manner. Because I was the captain's wife, I was offered the most desirable part of the fish, a delicacy set aside for the elite and presented to persons of high-ranking status—the snout. It was quite putrid. I demurred as politely as I could and chose a slice of the fresh fish, which was for inferior guests. When it came time to take our leave, we were well pleased to be rid of the civilities of the company.

In need of a walk, we had a delightful row around the bay to see if we could detect any spot which looked promising. Usually, we would find one or two rugged trails, but here there did not appear to be many suitable places. We stopped at the village and many of the residents came out of their houses to greet us. Some presented us with wonderful gifts of cranberries, which were large and well-flavoured. Others invited us into their houses, which, although humble, were neatly attired and well looked after. As we went about on our walk, the children of the village ran to us and bent down to kiss the hems of our clothing and grabbed our hands to kiss them as well. Our little William garnered a great deal of attention from the children, who would come up and caress him, perhaps because he was so foreign to them. In any case, he was glad enough to frolic and play with the children, as adults had been his only companions while on board the ship. The girls were very pretty and the women polite and cheerful. I was not as favourably impressed with the men, however. They seemed to be less clever than their wives. We had many pleasant walks during our stay, but we took care to land at a distance from the town. We preferred scrambling up the rocks to the annoyance of being followed. We were not used to people nor the attention and found such congregations unsettling.

The entertaining went on daily during our time in Awatcha Bay. We hosted many dinners and made sure our guests were served plenty of wine, beer, brandy, and rum, which they seemed to like. They did not have their own liquors except for something they called Quass, made from fermented rye bread. It tasted a bit like mead. While we were still at anchor, several other ships arrived, all fully dressed in their flags. As each ship entered and then departed, they fired their cannons as a salute: first to Empress Catherine, then once for each of the dignitaries on land, and then again for each of the ships in the harbour and their officers, and whoever else they could think of, sometimes firing fifteen rounds for each person. It made for an ear-splitting cacophony of clatter and left our part of the bay choked with smoke. We had never experienced so much camaraderie, feasting, and music. Our small ship was visited morning, noon, and night with our guests eating us out of house and home. In some cases, Captain Barkley's generosity was misunderstood and they thought they could take from the ship whatever they fancied. Although, upon reflection, this happened in many of the places we had visited. Such ceremonies, however, are an important part to securing permission to engage in trade.

Our trip did not prove successful. We had sailed all this long way and endured many hardships to trade for furs. The governor did bring us gifts of furs. I was presented with ten fine red fox skins called Shevadowsky's, Captain Barkley was given a very handsome otter skin, and William was given two sable skins from the governor's son. But despite our best efforts, the trade in pelts was non-existent.[1] To bypass government regulations against foreign trade in furs, transactions regularly took place in secrecy. It was our great misfortune that the governor was in residence at the time we arrived. It was his duty to prevent the Kamchadals (the Indigenous people of the land) from engaging in any commercial undertakings. Major Ismailov was aware that we came to trade, but despite the seeming friendship, the showering of small gifts, and our extravagant entertaining, we left with our stores greatly reduced and empty handed. It came clear to us that nothing was to be done in the way of trade, so we left the bay on July 20 and sailed farther south. We were glad to escape the endless ceremonies, the civility, and the noise, but we were disheartened to have left empty handed.

21

Furs, Deserters, and Warriors in Alaska

WE WERE TWENTY-SEVEN days at sea when, on August 16, we saw the icy peak of Mount St. Elias soaring above the clouds, looking like a regal potentate surveying its mountain kingdom.[1] This whole chain of mountains was unlike anything I had seen before. On August 18, we spotted Mount Fairweather, which is about 152 miles south of Mount St. Elias.[2] This part of the coast was unknown to us, so we had to tread carefully.[3] The weather was changeable, windy, and misty at times, but overall, it was tolerably warm. We were farther north than Captain Barkley intended, but we came across a sound called Admiralty Bay, where we found a secure anchorage in Lord Mulgrave's Harbour, east of the entrance.[4] It was sheltered and put us in the lee of a pretty island that was green and pleasant to the eye. Scanning the horizon, we spied several canoes that looked to have been out on a fishing expedition. As they drew closer, we could see that the men wore daggers suspended from their necks and carried spears with large sharp iron barbs. Their hair was matted and well-oiled

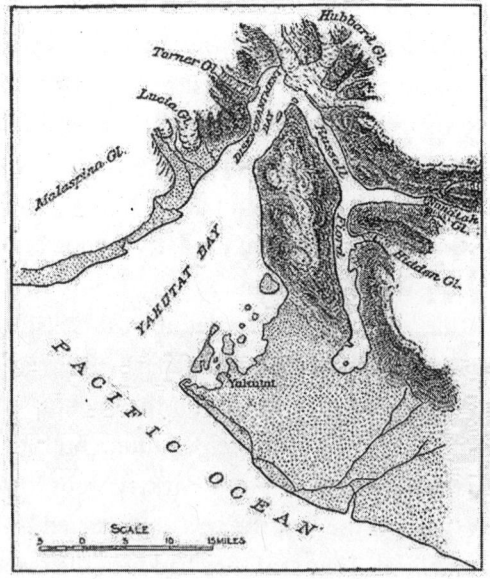

Map of Yakutat Bay and its Dependencies, 1910, by Gilbert Grove.
COURTESY FRESHWATER AND MARINE IMAGE BANK

and daubed with ochre. They dressed in sea otter skins that were stitched together and draped over their shoulders, but they wore nothing underneath their capes, leaving them quite exposed.[5] The women, on the other hand, were modestly dressed in skin dresses with a kind of woven rug thrown over their shoulders. Their hair was neatly parted in the middle, kept smooth behind their ears, and tied at the top in a knot. They also sported a bone or wood appendage that was slipped into a slit below the bottom lip.[6] Both men and women alike covered their faces with soot and red ochre. We found them to be astute traders who knew the worth of their furs. They sold us the furs they had with them, even the ones they were wearing.

I spent my days exploring the island and found the ground cultivated with oats, peas, and strawberries that were planted in amongst coarse grass. I thought it a bit surprising as the people looked to be unsettled, perhaps using the area as a seasonal stopover. The men gave us fish and the women provided us with different kinds of berries, fresh and dried, but the raspberries were especially delicious. It was a treat to eat fresh food and we relished it whenever we got the opportunity.

After putting everything in order aboard the ship and filling the water butts, we prepared for our departure. It was now July 25. As the crew was getting ready to haul the anchor, we saw a brig enter the sound. Initially we were delighted, but our excitement turned to suspicion when Captain Barkley went to render them assistance. While on the way, he was approached by a boat with four sailors on board. They said they had seen the mast of our ship and had been dispatched by Captain Hancock, last out of China, to seek provisions. They were woefully short of supplies. This was not an uncommon request by those that were far from their home port; bad weather and misadventure held many a ship to ransom. We gave them what they needed and wished them good voyage. Once again, we readied our ship for sail when we saw the same four reappear. They said their ship had left. We waited three days for it to return, but when that did not happen, we realized these sailors had either deserted or had been set adrift. As they were able-bodied seamen, we added them to our crew and told them we would see them off once we reached China.

It had been calm in our anchorage, but as the *Halcyon* turned out to sea we were welcomed by a violent wind and steep seas. With great effort, the sails were reefed and we stood offshore to ride out the storm. When the weather calmed somewhat, we ran for Cape Edgecumbe. Despite the weather, the scenery along this coast was breathtaking, truly a landscape painted by angels. The scale and breadth of the icy-capped mountains command attention. They are the rulers of their kingdom. As we neared the cape, the cliffs darkened to an inky black then slowly blended into a greyish white as we moved farther south. The coastline was striated with precipitous cliffs that dropped straight into the ocean. Along the shoreline, where the land and sea clashed, dangerous shoals poked up from the detritus left by erosion. We took a thrashing all the way down the coast. After another terrible night of rough seas, we rounded the cape and found a safe anchorage in Norfolk Sound and tucked into a cove at the bottom of the bay.[7] It was a relief to finally be away from the crashing sound of breaking waves and the fear that invokes. You never quite get over the anxiety that comes with such violence, although you learn to live with the dangers the ocean presents. For our dear William, severe weather events were of no consequence. He knew no other life, having spent most of his four years at sea.

From the ship, we could see there was habitation on shore that appeared to be of a more permanent nature than we found in Lord Mulgrave's Harbour. We were not surprised, then, when several large, well-appointed canoes visited us the next day. They were familiar with merchant ships such as ours and they brought sea otter skins to trade. We found the transaction for the pelts arduous and costly. Gunpowder and shot were first on their list, but strangely, they were not particularly interested in obtaining guns. It appeared that each canoe already had two or three muskets. They told us they preferred the accuracy of their spears over guns. Next on their list were blankets, cooking utensils, tools, and other iron weapons. A great advantage for us this time was that Captain

Barkley was able to understand and communicate with the traders. He had a great aptitude for languages and regularly studied
the languages of the peoples we met on our trips.

The women here had the same mouthpiece as did the women
we met in Admiralty Bay, except theirs were bigger. The ornaments
worn by the elderly women in the community were such a size they
had to support their bottom lip with their hands. The appendage allowed the women to be able to close their mouths, but only
with great difficulty. Eating was attended to with great effort. They
would toss their food into the back of their mouth, then throw
their head back with a jerk to make sure food would not get lodged
in the concave indentation of their lip. Here, too, the women supplied us with fresh wild berries that were juicy and sweet. None we
received were cultivated, as in Admiralty Bay.

The men projected a fierceness in their attitude, and we remained
wary. When on board, they took anything that was not put away,
and when our crew ventured on shore, they were stripped of all
they had, including their clothing, at times under gunpoint. On
one lovely moonlit evening Captain Barkley heard chanting, like a
war song. Through his night glass he saw several canoes tight into
the shoreline. It was quite frightening as we were not well manned.
As a warning, the ship's cannons were fired off over their heads.
The next day they came out to us attired in their war regalia, their
paddling timed to their chanting. They circled the *Halcyon* three
times. Tension mounted, but we remained calm. Suddenly, with
a great shout they pulled off their masks and proceeded to trade.
We were greatly relieved. Captain Barkley had always attempted
to treat those we met with respect and honour. They said they
had been on a raid the previous night and sold us the furs they
obtained. Had we stayed longer, I have no doubt that we would

have had an excellent cargo of sea otter skins. Unfortunately, we could not extend our stay as originally planned because we were running short of provisions from all the entertaining that took place in Kamskatcha. We were so completely fleeced that we were reduced to an allowance of a teacupful of rice a day until we could stop for more provisions. Fortunately, there was plenty of grog so there was no murmuring on board. As it was, Captain Barkley purchased a pretty good lot. It was not what we hoped, but at least we had some pelts to take back to Canton.

22

Under Attack
in Owyhee

WE LEFT FOR Owyhee on October 4, and after a month-long tedious voyage across the North Pacific, we made land on November 7. Our intention was to restock our supplies and sail on to Nootka to meet up with the *Venus*. We had heard that the *Venus* had been spotted by Captain George Vancouver in the Queen Charlotte Islands in the latter part of June, which was great news. Captain Shepherd and the crew were well. Perhaps we would see them next in Canton.

On this trip, we found a very different Owyhee than that of our last visit, five years ago. We were pleased to see that the pair of turkeys we presented had survived and were proliferating, although disappointingly we were not offered one for our stores. We were given to understand that the turkeys were so highly prized they were used solely as peace offerings, handed from one chief to another.

While here, we met Kaiana, the chief who had sailed from Cochinchina with Captain Meares and had tended to Winée on her deathbed. We found our meeting with him strained and were

A Canoe of the Sandwich Islands, the Rowers Masked, 1784, engraved by
Charles Grignion after John Webber. HONOLULU MUSEUM OF ART 11815.51

distrustful of him. Despite Captain Meares's trust in him, we
thought him a great rascal.[1] On the other hand, it was good to
visit again with Kamehameha. I was surprised to find that age
had softened him. He was more open and cheerful, and still as
generous and kind as when we first met him. He was now about
thirty-four years of age and had been in many wars since our last
visit. He was revered as a great warrior and was now king of the
island of Owyhee and part of the island of Maui.[2]

We had planned to spend time at anchor in Caracasoa Bay, taking on water and provisions, but were warned not to do so. There
had been attacks by both traders and Kānaka on each other, and
had we stayed, we would have been in great danger. There were two
other ships in the area, and we thought it would be best to group
together for protection. We met up with Captain Joseph Ingraham

89

from the brig *Hope* and Captain James Magee of the *Margaret*, both out of Boston. We set sail for Whitaty Bay on the island of Olowalu. We found the provisions less abundant than in Caracasoa Bay, but we did manage to fill our water butts and take on live hogs, yams, sugar cane, melons, and other fresh fruit.

On November 10, a Saturday, Captains Magee and Ingraham were on board with us enjoying a lively conversation accompanied by a delicious meal served with goblets of wine, when at around 3:00 PM, we were alerted to an impending attack upon the *Halycon*. The order was given for all hands to be on deck. We ran out to see a blazing apparition heading directly toward us. Of all the mishaps on a ship, fire was the most feared. We carried sufficient black powder, tar, pitch, and alcohol with us to create an explosion. In this moment, chaos reigned. We had to manoeuvre around all our freshly supplied livestock and stores that were stowed on deck. We didn't have time to raise the anchor, so in fear for our lives, Captain Barkley commanded the crew to cut the cable and hoist the sails. We put out to sea immediately, along with the *Hope* and *Margaret* following close behind. To perish now after all we had been through did not bear thinking about. After we gathered ourselves and were safely at sea, Captain Barkley reasoned that, as it was late in the year, rather than sailing on to Nootka to obtain more furs, the best choice for us would be to chart a course directly back to China. He wanted to avoid being the last ship of the season, as by then the market would be saturated and the price we could get for our furs greatly reduced.

23

Palanquins and Royalty in Cochinchina

OUR TRIP ACROSS the North Pacific took us a little over a month. I have almost no recollection of that time. I assume it was an uneventful trip. The coast near Macao does experience northeast monsoons from December to April, but I can't say we were affected in any way. As I age, I find my memory picking up and dropping treads without my permission. Fortunately, I came across some notes I had written about our time in Saigon so am able to provide more detail. I do know it was just a few days before Christmas, around December 23 or 24, that we set our anchor in the bay near Macao. We were just in time to celebrate Christmas and welcome in the new year of 1793. We learned that the *Venus* had arrived in China a day before we did. They had not done well obtaining furs in Nootka and the price they received for what they did bring back was poor. The original plan was to make two more trips, but there were now so many vessels in the trade that the markets were overwhelmed. Additionally, the cost of mounting such ventures was no longer profitable for us. Captain Barkley was determined

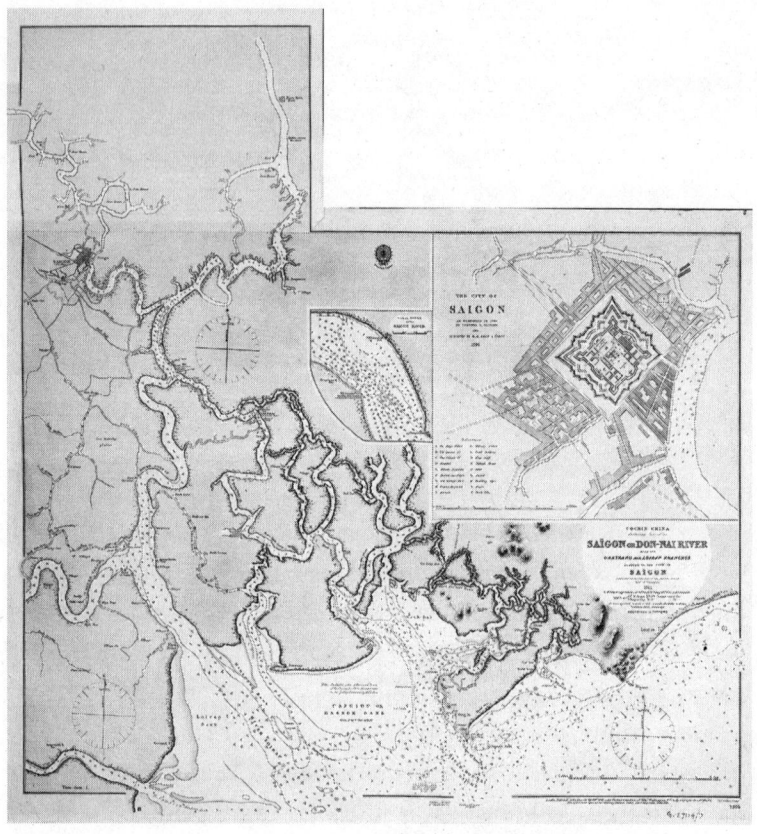

Admiralty Chart 1269, Cochin China and Don-Nai River, 1861,
by Captain Jean Marie Dayot. J. & C. WALKER. ROYAL MUSEUMS
GREENWICH CHARTS AND MAPS. PD-ART/PD-OLD-100

to take the principal part of our cargo to Bengal, where Russian
agents were buying up furs.

We stayed in Macao until February 25. Nine days later, on
March 6, we sighted Cape St. James and the entrance to the great
Mekong River Delta. As we rounded the peninsula, we found a

good anchorage about a mile inside in the bay. Before we could voyage up the river to Saigon, we first had to attend to customs, which took over two hours. It was never a straightforward procedure of simply providing the required documents. Convention decreed that it was necessary to afford libations to the satisfaction of the port officials who came aboard before they examined our paperwork. We then had another six hours to wait for the tide to turn, which began shortly after low water. At spring tide, the river runs at about five knots, which will push a ship backward, and nothing but absolute necessity will induce the local people to stem the tide. Leaving the *Halcyon* at anchor, we travelled up the river in a small vessel that was in an abysmal condition. Besides being dirty, it was extremely uncomfortable. It was not a short trip. Saigon is twenty-four leagues (sixty-two nautical miles) up the Dong Nai River. As we were winding our way along the river, we could see that it would be very easy to get lost in the delta as there were multiple branches, rendering a confusing network of channels that seemed to go any which way. By the time we disembarked from that unpleasant journey, it had been nearly twenty-four hours since leaving Cape St. James. We were tired and had no idea where to lodge. We chose not to take up residence in the town as we knew nothing about the accommodations and were a bit uncertain of Saigon itself. As chance would have it, we were offered quarters aboard the brig *Mary* that belonged to Mr. Gumbou. We were generously entertained by the captain, who kindly provided us with the use of his own cabin. From the ship, we had an unobstructed view of the town. Laid out before us was a long street, attractively lined with young mango trees. Toward the back of the town was a citadel in the shape of an octagon. It appeared to be recently constructed. In the centre of the citadel was a large square divided by

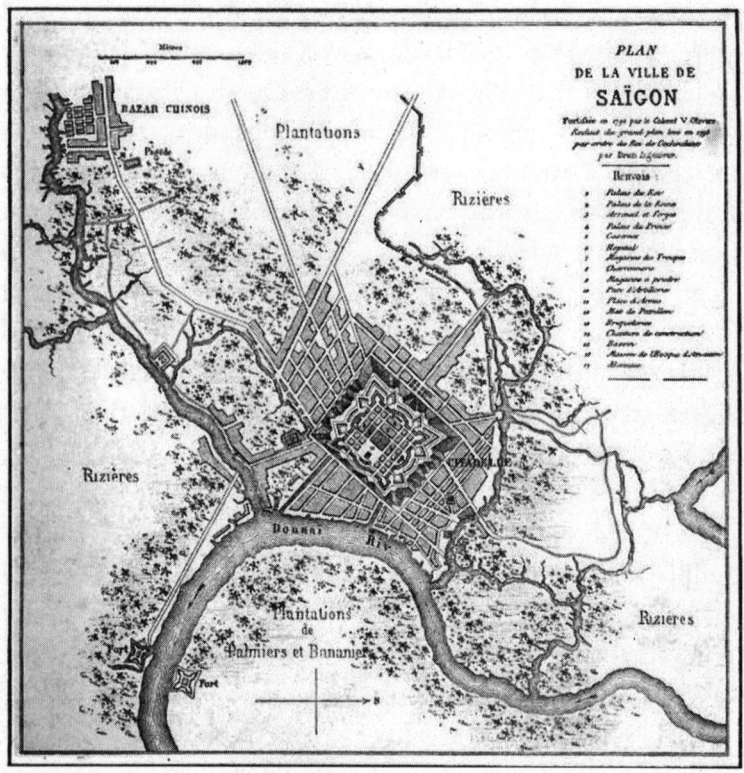

Map of Saigon, 1860. PD-OLD-70

four roads, each lined with trees that led up to the gate of the royal palace. It was well fortified with armaments and was supplied with provisions of every sort, in case of another siege. This area had a fractious existence and had been recently devastated by civil wars.

Captain Barkley was invited by a group of French residents in the city to meet with them and with a French missionary of great standing. I chose to stay aboard, but news travels quickly in small places, and the palace, upon hearing a European woman was visiting, invited me through a deputation sent from the king, Gia Long (Nguyễn Ánh), to visit the ladies of his family.[1] I was hesitant to leave the security of the ship on my own, but was informed that the invitation was considered a great honour and that every preparation was made to welcome me and our son. I wore my best dress, a plain affair made of white Bengal muslin accented by a wide ribbon sash that dropped to the ground. The dress itself had a long train attached. It was in style in Europe, but I fear too plain for a royal visit. As we stepped on shore, the king's son was there to greet us. He was a shy fourteen-year-old, dressed in a regal manner with a robe of rich brocade embroidered with a dragon, particular to the next heir to the throne. I would say he was pretty in appearance. One of the king's palanquins was ready to receive us. Before we embarked, we were greeted with a type of high-pitched music, which I had never heard before. The discordance so terrified me that for a time I was overcome and felt unable to walk. Surrounding us was a contingent of twenty of the king's men, ready with whips at their side to protect us from the throngs of people that turned out to catch their first glimpse of a European woman and child. With such grandeur, we were carried through the streets to the palace. The palanquin had a sort of rocking motion set by the cadence of the carriers. Fortunately, I was used to such modes of transportation as palanquins were used all over Macau, although none so grand as this one.

Upon our arrival, the young prince guided us through the palace to visit the with the king's mother, sister, and wife. I was given a stool to sit on, three steps below the king's mother. She was an older woman, about the age of sixty, and did not display any sense of grandeur in her dress or her demeanour. Nevertheless, she was paid great respect by the other women there. William sat on the floor surrounded with toys that were put there for his amusement. The king and other men and women of the household were present but remained sequestered behind a screen. We were served coffee, sweetmeats, and fruit. Communication was challenging as the young prince, as well as the interpreter, had great difficulty with French. The translator was so anxious that he prostrated himself on the floor with every sentence. I understood very little Portuguese, so I fear their questions were badly answered. Much of our interaction was through gestures, which offered each party only the most cursory information about the other. I wondered what they were thinking about us and how they saw us. I do know they were intrigued by my hair and were surprised to find that it curled, while William's hair was perfectly straight. William became the centre of attention: they caressed his face, examined his clothes, and touched his hair. He loved it and enjoyed himself as he rolled around on the floor tossing the beautifully hand-stitched cushions about. I had trouble getting him to behave. I was relieved when it was time to depart. To my surprise, rather than being returned to the ship as I had hoped, we were taken to the homes of various dignitaries in the town. Inside each home, we were entertained in a similar manner as that of the palace, replete with music and food. It was very intense and exhausting, and certainly taxed the abilities of a five-year old. It was foolish to hope that William would be able to maintain any sense of decorum after such expansive attention. Being the first European woman invited to the royal palace, and as a captain's wife, I had to be approachable and yet present myself with manners and bearing. Something I always tried to do, hopefully with success.

CHAPTER 24

Pirates and War

WE LEFT SAIGON later in March and headed south to Mauritius, intending to stop in to see our friends and enjoy a relaxed respite before we carried on to Bengal.[1] We were in the South China Sea heading toward the Singapore Strait when we were ambushed by local pirates. This area was well known for piracy as there are so many islands with inlets in which to hide. Our ship was boarded, the crew tied up, and Captain Barkley, William, and I were taken ashore as prisoners. We were terrified as to what they might do to us. All mariners have heard stories of sailors who had been brutalized at the violent hands of their captors, sometimes with tragic outcomes ending with losing one's head. We were told to sit on the ground. The women of the village came out and crowded around, pressing ever closer to us. They stared at us for some time, talking rapidly amongst themselves. I pulled William closer into me for his protection and in the hopes of keeping him calm. They then reached for my hair and started pulling out all of the pins I used to keep it in an upsweep. When my hair fell to its full length, which by now was quite long, they seemed alarmed. I assume it was the colour they found disconcerting. They gasped and stepped back.

From their reaction I presumed they thought I was some sort of supernatural being, not human. Luck was on our side. After more discussion, they released us and took us back to our ship. It was a terrifying experience and a narrow escape. Once back on board, we departed immediately before they changed their minds.[2] Still shaken, we slipped through the Singapore Strait and headed to Mauritius.[3]

When you spend years at sea, in many cases at the outer reaches of the known world, you lose touch with political and social issues that seem important to those who live on land. Most of your time is cloaked in your own world, where the dominant aspects of your life are the wind, the sea state, and survival. Thus, when we sailed south, we were completely unaware that privateers and French corsairs had stepped up their raids on merchant ships in the Indian Ocean. They were most active around the Malabar Coast, the Sunda and Malacca Straits, and the Bay of Bengal, just where we had been. Their frigates were fast and could easily out sail most merchant ships. The only safe way for us to travel under such conditions was in large convoys, but as we were not on the normal spice trade circuit, we were on our own. Although we were ignorant as to the current escalation, the Indian Ocean was always an area that we travelled with caution. As we sailed further south, putting distance between ourselves and the pirates' lairs, we thought we had escaped further misfortunes. However, when we entered Port Louis, we sailed right into the heart of their home base. The *Halcyon* was captured on June 6, 1793, and we were held as prisoners for a year. It was only through the kind intervention of friends that we were allowed to stay at the home of Anne Joseph Hippolyte de Maurès, comte de Malartic, the governor of the Îsle de France Chalian de la Chelaignien, rather than in a makeshift prison. At the time, he was also the Commandant General of the French Establishments beyond the Cape of Good Hope. He was quite accomplished in warfare and had fought on the Plains of Abraham in New France, an area in the world we had not visited. He was a man of great reserve, was well respected in the community, and helped tame some of the tension evident there.

The gaiety and relaxed ambience we so enjoyed in Mauritius now had a strained mood, undercut by revolutionary angst. The French were preparing for a pending war with Britain and the Dutch Republic. What no one knew in our part of the world was that, by February, war had already been declared.[4] That information did not reach Mauritius until early July. France wanted to take over the valuable East Indian trade, and war spurred them on to parry and thrust their way through the British merchant fleet. The fighting in the Indian Ocean became intense and merchant shipping was seriously curtailed. The privateers that were in Mauritius formed a cooperative. They sailed with "letters of marque" provided by the French government, which granted them permission to seize and sell any foreign merchant ships they came across as well as their cargo. Once they captured a ship, the surviving crew were either never heard of again or were taken as prisoners of war. Privateering was an extremely lucrative business and a great boon to the economy of Mauritius and the French Navy. American, Dutch, British, Arab, and Indian ships were brought into port as prizes of war.[5] The *Princess Royal*, for example, was captured by three French privateers on September 29, 1793, off the Sunda Strait and brought into Mauritius. It was a great prize and consequently was subject to a bidding war and sold for 2,400,000 livres. She was then put back in service for the French under the name *Duguay Trouin* and was used to patrol the Bay of Bengal.[6]

At the same time, a Dutch East Indiaman was brought into port and sold for 600,000 livres, and her cargo for another 800,000 livres. Even our old sailing companion, the *Venus,* was involved. It was on a course from Batavia via Penang and reported witnessing the taking of a Dutch East Indiaman in Sunda Strait by a French privateer. The Dutch ship was carrying cargo rich in spices and gold dust, which was what the privateers were keen to obtain.[7] The effect of all of this was that the cost of living for necessities rose in Mauritius. In protest, an angry mob of citizens raised a gallows in front of Government House with a sign that read, ACCAPAREURS, VOILA VOTRE RECOMPENSE, "Monopolists, here is your reward."[8] It was not a pleasant scene to witness and reinforced the strain that pervaded the island.

25

America Bound

AFTER A YEAR of enforced detention, we were released. We packed up our few belongings and took passage on the *Betsy*, an American ship bound for Newport on the eastern coast of America. Again, I don't remember much about the trip, but I do know that as soon as we arrived, we made our way to New York, where Captain Barkley used the remains of his capital to purchase a brig to continue in our trade. The *Amphion* was a humble ship; it certainly wasn't in the best of shape and Captain Barkley needed to have it refitted at further expense. After the necessary repairs were completed to my husband's satisfaction, we purchased our supplies and secured a cargo, which I think might have been cotton. I can't remember exactly. We were going across the Atlantic to England, but as we were arranging to set out, we found out that the authorities would not allow a foreign national to sail as captain in an American ship from an American port. Captain Barkley was required to find someone who could take his place, which added to our expenses. My husband was an excellent navigator and captain and was not favourably disposed to hand over command of his ship to another captain, particularly someone he did not know. Finally, with our paperwork secured, we left in November of 1794 under the command of Captain Sayer sailing under American colours.[1]

CHAPTER

26

To England,
Robbery

IT WAS LATE December 1794 when we spotted Penzance, the entrance to the English Channel. That meant we were only eighty miles from Poole. It was with a great sigh of relief that we rounded the Sandbanks Peninsula, sailing between it and Brownsea Island and spotting the Tudor-style castle on the island that guards the entrance to the harbour. Bringing a ship into port is always a busy and exciting time. The lookouts were at their posts, the sail master was occupied ensuring the lines and sails were properly stowed, leaving just enough canvas to take us gently alongside. The deckhands readied the ropes for docking, and as we drew near, the longboat was dispatched to take the messenger lines to the mooring capstans on the dock. After we berthed, we had to tamper our excitement and busy ourselves with ensuring the ship was secured before we could go ashore. Anxious to surprise our families for Christmas, we left the *Amphion* in the hands of Captain Sayer with the understanding Captain Barkley would return immediately after the festivities to unload our cargo. We had no idea when we disembarked that it would be a very long time before we saw the *Amphion* again. In blissful ignorance of the villainous actions of the devious American captain, we bounced along the rutted road in a carriage to London to spend Christmas with our families. We hoped there might be a goose and some delectable, sweet jellies to delight in for our Christmas meal.

We took lodgings in Norfolk Street, Strand. My husband was so pleased to be able to visit with his brother. The last we saw of him was when we left India for our "short" trip, which turned out to be several years and quite an ordeal. My beloved husband and his brother were very close. John, being eleven years the senior, looked upon his younger brother as a father would toward his son. I was still reserved toward John, having never quite forgiven him for meddling in our plans to stay in India in the country trade. My family was here too, and I was very sad to learn that my father had died in Ostend eleven months previously, never knowing of our fate nor meeting his grandchild. It seemed so many years ago when I waved goodbye to him as we slipped our lines at the dock in Ostend and set sail for adventures that I never could have imagined.

While William and I stayed in London, Captain Barkley returned to the *Amphion* to discharge our cargo and take care of the ship's business. When he reached Poole, the Amphion was nowhere to be seen. To his utter dismay, the said American captain had absconded with the ship, fully loaded with its the cargo and remaining stores. With single-minded intent, my beloved husband set out immediately to find the ship with the help of his brother John. Enquiries were made and trips taken to various seaports, where it was rumoured the *Amphion* had been spotted. After an exhaustive search Captain Barkley heard of a promising account that the *Amphion* had been seen on the other side of the Atlantic. Once more, he set off across the ocean, as a passenger on board the *Ocean*. When he finally found the *Amphion*, all the cargo and stores had been sold off and Captain Sayer had kept possession of the brig and freighted her for his own purpose. It was but one more devastating financial blow. Captain Barkley got the *Amphion* out of Sayer's clutches after much trouble and returned to England, arriving the very day that our dear Jane was born, January 18, 1796. Without any earnings, we were forced to live like itinerant travellers, spending time in leased houses. Eventually we moved in with John and his wife, Elizabeth, at their home in the Princes Building in Bath. They had no children of their own, so they looked upon our growing family with delight. Despite their kindness and staunch financial support, the debt laid very heavily in my dear husband's thoughts. He was always looking for ways in which to earn our keep.

27

Captain Barkley's Last Command

AN OPPORTUNITY WAS presented in 1809, when Captain Barkley was offered the chance to take the *Venus* on a trading voyage bound for the coasts of Chile, Peru, and Mexico.[1] There was some suggestion that he would then travel across the Pacific to Botany Bay in Australia. Despite the advice of his brother to the contrary, my dear husband chose to take advantage of the offer. We had spent fifteen miserable years living with his brother, in Bath for the winter season and Halliford House in Sunbury during the summers. It was not a situation to our liking, but we endured that time for the sake of the children. I doubt that John understood his brother's need to support his family on his own. John Barkley was a wealthy man and did not consider any expenses for our family as unworthy. However, my husband was a talented and prideful man and preferred being in a position of command over his own destiny. What he had not really considered was the fact that his health had not been good, and at sixty-three years of age, he was not as agile or energetic as he once was. It did give him pause for

TOP Halliford House, Home of the Barkleys, n.d.
COURTESY SUNBURY AND SHIPPERTON LOCAL HISTORY SOCIETY

BOTTOM Halliford House, drawn by Martha Shaw, n.d.
COURTESY OF MADELEINE SYMES AND COURTESY OF
SUNBURY AND SHIPPERTON LOCAL HISTORY SOCIETY

thought, but the chance of earning an income outweighed such concerns. We had been apart from each other for short times in our marriage, particularly when he was looking for the *Amphion*, but it was something we never got used to. My dear husband wrote to us at every opportunity and his letters were filled with loving remarks and queries about me and the children. His letters were welcoming as I was dreadfully ill at the time, confined to my bed with a rheumatic fever.

It was while he was stuck in Buenos Aires, Argentina, for more than two months that he made the agonizing decision to give up the venture. He wrote that the *Venus* was in dreadful shape and unseaworthy. The supercargoes wanted him to take the *Venus* around Cape Horn westbound, which meant he would be sailing against the prevailing winds. If he couldn't make it, he would have to reroute east toward Tahiti, far from his destination. In either case, the *Venus*, in its current state, would not stand up to the rigors of the ocean temperament. The caulking had been completely neglected, the cells were rotten, there was no oakum between the staves, the rigging was in tatters and full of splices, and the ratlines were so old that it was impossible to send anyone up on them to square the sails or work on repairs. Another major issue of concern was that Spain had been repossessed by the French, who were set against the British, which put my husband in a difficult situation. The supercargoes were only concerned with their cargo and over a discussion about the situation during an evening meal, Captain Barkley was told to fire upon any Spanish ships at first sighting. As master of the ship and someone well skilled in the art of trade, Captain Barkley balked at that advice and told them so. He said that in peaceable times it was a delicate thing to be the aggressor and he would be reluctant to fire on any Spanish boats on their coasts unless they attacked with hostile intent. He explained that such an action would destroy the objective of the trip, which was always to trade with a good understanding. They were livid that he questioned their authority in such matters and told him that not only was he was not fit to command the *Venus* as he had not been at sea for many years, but he was too old to do so. It was obvious to my husband they did not want a highly skilled captain and a talented navigator, but rather someone who was a rough, plain sailor and would abide by advice from people who had never been to sea. Captain Barkley felt that he was but a mere cypher, a sailing master, with the superintendents and supercargoes assuming all the power, even though they had no knowledge of the sea; one of the supercargoes was a linen draper and the other a decayed wine merchant. They were not his employers, but as they travelled with him, they made his life miserable. It also did not help that his chief mate proved to be a snake in the grass and often colluded with one or the other of the supercargoes against Captain Barkley. My husband said that the chief mate was disagreeable and was continuously quarreling with someone about anything, and when discussion became heated, he flew down to his cabin for protection.

Captain Barkley also realized that he had been greatly deceived about the proposed mercantile success of the venture. It became apparent that it was not possible to get the kind of prices for the cargo as he had been led to believe. There was plenty of conversation with commanders and officers who had their ships seized but were fortunate enough to have escaped. They relayed stories of the dangers that awaited merchant ships along that stretch of coastline, and that both Chile and Peru were in disarray and given over to bandits of every sort. The likelihood of being able to discharge the ship's cargo was slim to none, and the chances of evading pirates was low. These pirates, they also reported, were a bad set who, upon capturing a ship, would gladly kill its officers and crew without a care, or alternately hold them hostage for years at a time.

Because of the constant nattering of the supercargoes, my dear husband wrote, he really thought sometimes that he should jump overboard. He was deeply vexed about the situation, which then brought on an attack of nerves that was subsequently attended by a bout of ill health. His situation was already compromised from a fall he'd had off a ladder as he was going onto the poop deck, which was riddled with dry rot. Initially, he had been pleased with the idea of earning a few hundred pounds, but he realized that under the circumstances, continuing was a near impossibility. Disheartened, he reluctantly resigned his commission. The owners of the ship accepted my husband's submission to quit the venture and said they were perfectly satisfied with him and wished for no other commander but understood and asked if he could find them another captain, which he did. He felt that he let down not only himself, but the rest of his family. In a letter to his brother, he wrote, "Without you, my family & me must long ago have felt the severe hand of want. Yet I am sure you never intended I should lose an opportunity of doing something to advantage if it offered, at the same time leaving it in my own breast to choose the path... How often have you, my Dearest brother, told me to remain quiet, make my Mind easy, look to the education of my children. I should never want anything. Would to God I had done so."[2]

Epilogue

FOR YEARS, MY children have pleaded with me to chronicle our life at sea. In so doing, I realize that despite our many hardships, Captain Barkley and I had an extraordinary life. For one who came from a somewhat cloistered life, the experiences of facing the challenges of the sea, meeting so many people, and visiting places that few from this side of the world had ever seen were transformative. I grew from being a young, naive girl into a strong, self-contained woman. My children tell me that I sometimes exhibit a temper. Perhaps it developed during those years when our very existence and livelihood were too often driven by providence. Those years were exciting, and I gained experiences and an understanding about the human spirit that pushed the bounds of my thinking. But now in my old age, I am content. I miss my husband terribly. Our love for each other was profound; his deterioration during his last years was difficult to witness. We all have infirmities as we age—he was seventy-three, after all—but acknowledgement of that fact is not the same as bearing witness of a loved one whose body is failing them. He had been feeling irritable and fretful for some time as his health was unstable. He gradually worsened, and then in 1831, he had that terrible fall. The children and I were all upstairs and heard an alarming thump. We ran downstairs as fast as we could and there was Papa at the bottom, lifeless. We thought we had lost him, but the doctor came immediately and was able to revive him. He had injured his head quite severely and subsequently had a series of seizures. We stayed by his side while the doctor applied leeches to his temples in the hopes of preventing further convulsions. We were all so relieved when he recovered, but he was never the same again and his overall health continued a downward trend. His meandering ups and downs kept us in a state of constant alarm. During the latter part of his life, I was not well myself. I realized I had lost weight and suffered from bouts of gout. Ill health seemed to run a steady course in our family, moving from one to another and back again. There were several times when Martha was so ill I thought we would lose her.[1] I was just recovering from another attack of gout when Papa took his last breath. I shall never forget the day; it happened on Thursday, May 17, in the year 1832. He was worn out more by care and sorrow than by years as he had been blessed with a very strong constitution. We buried him at Enfield in the vault at the side of our dear children, where I intend to join them when it shall please God to call me hence. We had been married forty-five years, five months, and one day, during which period we had experienced the vagaries of fortune and encountered great dangers, having been engaged in very perilous voyages together commencing with the ship *Loudoun* in 1786.

The other losses I have experienced sit heavy in my heart too. We were devastated when baby Patty died near Celebes, and then William Hippolyte, who shared our experiences at sea, died of scarlet fever at just fourteen years of age. There was the loss of our boy John, who we never got to know. He died when but a week old. There was William, who was born to us in 1805 but left us when he was twenty months old. To our children, know that your father loved all of you and fretted about you when he was away, always asking after each one of you and providing comfort if any of you were ill. I remember the long summer evening walks at Sunbury, with Papa, old Dash, and Martha. They would set off after the evening meal to watch the sun set and Martha would come back home all excited and tell me the same story each time. Just as the sun was about to set, they would begin the countdown—"going... going... gone"—until the sun disappeared below the horizon.

After Papa died, I had no reason to stay in Hertford, so I took a house in Warwick Road, Upper Clapton, to be near Martha and her children. I furnished it with what I had saved from the wreck at Hertford and the proceeds of the sale of the furniture and fixtures, the latter of which was a dead loss as the water closet alone cost £70.00. I left Hertford after having disposed of the lease of the house there together with the principal part of the furniture, which with the fitting up of the house and fixtures had cost £636.10. I only realised £221, including furniture I kept, which was deducted from the gross amount of the sale. I lost at least £415 by the transaction.

I seem to be wandering aimlessly, immersed in my recollections, making probably little sense. Therefore, I shall end here least my thoughts get diverted once again. My eyes are tired, and my gout is acting up. The rest, my dear family knows well. I feel fortunate in my life to have had a great love and to be surrounded by the love of my children, to which I add my delightful and many grandchildren.

* * *

IT WAS NOW late in the evening and Frances could feel the chill creeping throughout the room. The embers in the fireplace had long ago ceased flickering, the house was quiet. Her grandchildren were tucked snugly in their beds and Martha had long since departed for hers. She flipped back to the first page of the diary and, in her perfectly schooled penmanship, wrote the word "Reminiscences." Frances then put down her pen, her writing finished. Sitting alone in the darkness, she wept, the silent tears of a wife and mother who had lost and yet gained so much.[2]

Conclusion

FRANCES AND CHARLES had lost much since they first set sail as a newly married couple on their journey to make their fortune in the fur trade. They arrived home in England with little to show for their eight years employed as merchant sea traders. What monetary compensation they did have was depleted by Captain Barkley searching the world hoping to retake possession of his ship and its cargo and to right other injustices. Reduced to poverty, they spent many years living off the largess of Charles's brother John. Initially they lived with John and his wife, splitting the year between Princes Building in Bath and at Halliford House in Sunbury-on-Thames. The Halliford House, or Sunbury as they called it, had been in the Barkley family since 1777 and belonged to John, who had inherited it from his and Charles's uncle William Barkley, a wealthy London barrister who built the house in 1777 to use as his country estate. After John's death in 1822, it was passed to Charles and Frances.[1] Finding the upkeep expensive, they took their inheritance and purchased a lovely house on North Crescent in Hertford in June 1828. They had many happy times there, but still struggled financially and were sometimes provided with "emergency" monetary gifts from Charles's sister. They also received a small inheritance from Mr. Forbes, his cousin from India. The money was certainly a help and, as Martha said, "We struggled on rather better after that."[2] Success, however, cannot always be calculated in monetary terms. As a couple, they developed a deep love that would sustain them as they suffered through death and hardship, wonder and joy. "God forever bless you, the best of women," Charles wrote to his wife, and Frances always referred to Charles as, "my blessed husband."

The Barkleys lived a life filled with adventure, sailing to the outer edges of the world and to places where few Europeans had gone. They made discoveries and wrote about people, communities, and events that are now etched into annals of history. Importantly, they give us glimpses into the inter-sanctum of global trading, with its competing interests, territorial fractiousness, skullduggery, and unscrupulous behaviour of some players. Although filtered through the lens of British merchant seamen, we get time-stamped snippets of coastal peoples and islands in a time two hundred years in the past. Despite the loss of some of Captain Barkley's logs, there are sufficient recordings which added to seafaring knowledge of both coastal and deep-sea navigation in areas not well known or well-travelled by eighteenth century explorers and merchant traders. As a tangible legacy, the Barkleys' names have been memorialized on the west coast of Vancouver Island in Barkley Sound, and in inlets, channels, and capes in the vicinity. There is also a ship called the *Frances Barkley* that runs tours out of Ucluelet, and a street named after them in both Vancouver (Barclay Street) and in Victoria, British Columbia. Up a short steep hill in the seaside community of Oak Bay on Vancouver Island, a cairn sits atop Gonzales Hill with its unparalleled views of the Strait of Juan de Fuca. The cairn includes the names of early European navigators, including Captain Charles Barkley, who noted the Strait of Juan de Fuca. And on the island of Hawai'i, the Barkleys'

TOP Cairn atop Gonzales Hill, 2022. COURTESY OF THE AUTHOR

BOTTOM Outlook over the Strait of Juan de Fuca from Gonzales Hill, 2022. COURTESY OF THE AUTHOR

Conclusion

Martha (Patty) Shaw, née Barkley, n.d. COURTESY MADELEINE SYMES

gift of turkeys, although many generations since, still strut, gobble, cluck, and putter around freely.

Upon their return, their family grew and thrived, and their daily routines were much like others. Frances and Charles had seven children, losing three to early deaths. As their children grew, they stayed close to their families, visiting regularly. They had family spats and squabbles, particularly with their sixth child, Charles Frances Barkley, who caused them financial grief. In time, Frances went to live with her daughter Martha long after her husband's death. When Frances grew ill, Martha wrote, "How earnestly do I pray for her restoration but really I almost fear we shall not have her many years & after she is gone, I feel that I never can be *quite* happy again."[3] Frances died on May 22, 1845. She was predeceased by her son Charles Frances, who died of a most virulent case of typhus fever just ten days earlier, in a hotel in Germany.

In all, Frances and Charles Barkley had thirty-one grandchildren, eighty-five great-grandchildren, and 117 great-great-grandchildren. Their wanderlust was passed onto many in their family, with over half born outside of England, some on the Indian subcontinent and others in South Africa, Argentina, Sri Lanka, and Vancouver Island in British Columbia, Canada. Perhaps listening to the stories told by their grandparents kindled a yearning to explore worlds outside of their own. After her husband's death, Martha took their six children to live in France, Germany, Switzerland, Prague, and then Italy for their education. Her son, Robert Barkley Shaw, was an explorer and diplomat whose own life rivalled that of his grandmother. He travelled the Silk Road and was the first Englishman to visit some of the villages along the way. In 1872, the Royal Geographical Society awarded him the Patron's Gold Medal for his exploration of Eastern Turkestan (part of modern-day China) and for his astronomical observations. He was also awarded the position of the British Joint Commissioner at Ladakh in northern India between 1872 and 1877, and the British Resident at Mandalay in Upper Burma (central and northern Myanmar) in 1878.[4]

To this day, many of the Barkleys' descendants carry part of their famous relatives' names within their own, with Francis, Charles, Trevor, and Barkley being common. Frances's magnificent red hair that amazed many she met during her years at sea, and which saved their lives on a few occasions, is still resplendent throughout the generations.

Acknowledgements

I WOULD LIKE to honour my late husband, Captain Brian Silvester, Master Mariner, FNI, who was my champion and stood by my side through the many years that I put words on paper telling others' stories. His patient explanation of sailing routes, currents, winds, ship stability, the merchant sea trade, and all other things nautical have been an immense support in helping me to understand the life of a merchant seaman now and in the eighteenth century. Captain John Anderson, MM, a teller of sea stories in his own right, provided me with invaluable information on the history of ships' discipline. I have had the wonderful opportunity to connect with many of the Barkley and Trevor family descendants. The pride and esteem they hold of Charles and Frances are evident in all their correspondence with me. I would especially like to thank Phil and Helen Broomfield, now friends, who travelled from England to British Columbia to further explore the history of their famous relatives. Their research on the genealogies of the Barkleys and Trevors has been a very productive and a time-consuming passion for them, for which I am indebted. Another relative, Erica Utsi, helped put to rest the conventional lore that Charles Barkley's father had drowned in the Hooghly River. Together, we had fun unravelling the whereabouts of his untimely demise. Thanks also to Hallie Stanley, Adam Trevor, and

Jim Attwood for their research on the Barkleys and Trevors. The Barnes family of Vancouver Island, fifth and sixth generation Barkleys, alerted me to the fact that an intended replacement plaque for the cairn on Gonzales Hill, commemorating the exploration of the Strait of Juan de Fuca, left Captain Charles Barkleys name off and substituted Captain John Meares's name instead. The mistake was duly noted and rectified. It seems that even two hundred years later, Meares's duplicity is still in operation. Thanks also to Captain Poyntz and Captain Steele for helping with various points in navigation and listening patiently to me blather on about sailing routes during the eighteenth century. Behind every book is a hard-working team that is essential to its publication. Words cannot express how grateful I am to Lara Kordic for providing me the opportunity to share the story of this remarkable woman with others. To my very astute editor, Nandini Thaker, a wiz at punctuation, spelling, and unscrambling words and whose tireless reading and rereading, advice and cheery attitude kept me on the right path, I am in awe of her talent. I am indebted to Monica Miller whose enthusiasm and knowledge of marketing and publicity help to make this work accessible to readers. Although Frances left no images of herself, Kimiko Fraser created the perfect portrait for the cover of the book. Importantly, I owe a debt of gratitude to Rodger Touchie, publisher of Heritage House Publishing, and Pat Touchie, publisher emeritus of TouchWood Editions, who have, through their tireless efforts and love of Canadian history, created a platform by which we writers have been able to share the stories of amazing people who have been inspirational in the history of our country. Finally, I would like to acknowledge Beth Hill, whose writings have notably added to the rich history of British Columbia and is the inspiration behind this book.

Notes

Introduction

1 Captain Barkley began his training in 1770 as an apprentice in the merchant navy aboard his father's ship, the *Pacific*. He sailed under several masters, then at the age of twenty-six, he was given command of the *Loudoun* (renamed *Imperial Eagle*) in 1786.

2 Jeanne Baret, a Frenchwoman who sailed with Bougainville's expedition in 1763, can lay claim to being the first, but she sailed in disguise as a man, acting as the valet of Commerson, a scientist on the voyage. Although her shipmates had their suspicions, to acknowledge such would put the ship in contravention of French naval regulations. The earliest women at sea were probably stowaways. If their protector was of sufficiently high rank, they walked openly upon the decks. There are a few records concerning stowaway women, but in 1589, printed orders to the Spanish captains of the vessels of the Armada explicitly prohibited women on board and threatened severe punishment for anyone disobeying the order, clear evidence that the custom of hiding women below decks was an ancient one.

3 It was common practice for foreign explorers and voyagers to name places previously unknown to them for their country's rulers, notable people, ships, or members of their crew. They may or may not have been aware that oftentimes these lands had been inhabited for hundreds if not thousands of years and that the people there had their own names or markers for those places. The age of discovery is a misnomer; the age of contact is a better descriptor.

Chapter 1

1 Captain Barkley's father, also Captain Charles Barkley, went to sea in the service of the East India Company and was the captain of the Indiaman *Pacific*. Family lore has it that he died in the Hooghly River, but research done by Erica Utsi, a relative of the Barkleys, found that the *Pacific* was heading to Madras (Chennai) when Captain Barkley became ill with a fever and succumbed to his affliction six days later. The ship's log reads: "on Sunday the 14th Day of August At 3am Departed this life Captain Charles Barkley of a fever-having been ill Six Days Only—At Noon Committed the Body to the Deep." There was no fixed position recorded in the

log, but they were in sight of Friars Hood, a 658-metre peak now called Walimbe Hela, located in the Nuwaragala Hana forest reserve in Sri Lanka. The latitude and longitude for Friars Hood is 70°26'53"N/81°32'6"E. If one were to draw a line from Friars Hood, the nearest town by the ocean, one would come to Maruthamunai on the east coast of Sri Lanka, at the latitude and longitude of 70°26'24" N/81°49'29"E. Not knowing how far out at sea they were nor at what angle they were viewing Friars Hood, one can only get an approximation at best.

2   Reefing the sail refers to reducing the area of the sail in order to improve the stability of a ship during rough weather.

3   Frances does not write about what she used to soothe her husband, but it was common to minister such a mixture for a fever on board ships at the time.

Chapter 3

1   Frances does not mention if her husband taught her navigation, but her knowledge of weather makes it seem she at least learned the rudiments. She did, however, teach him French.

Chapter 4

1   One league is equal to three nautical miles. Nautical miles are used in maritime navigation and are not the same as a statute mile. One nautical mile is equal to 1.1508 of one land-based mile. Each nautical mile is equal to one degree of latitude.

2   Kanaka is singular, whereas Kānaka is plural.

3   While Frances does not mention how the Kānaka put iron to use, the facts are accurate and it's important to gain an understanding of the significance of iron to people who did not have the raw materials for its production. Before European traders came to their shores, they effectively fashioned tools out of bone, wood, and stone.

4   Frances does not mention her exact location, but it was mostly likely Kaena Point, the most western point of Oʻahu.

5   Perhaps during the initial stages of introduction, Frances heard the young woman referred to as wahine (wah-hee-neh), meaning "woman," and assumed that was her name. A more sensitive rendering would be ka wahine, meaning "the woman."

6   Historically, Hawaiians, although great explorers and masters of long-distance sea voyages, had surprisingly little contact with outside nations until the arrival of the European trading ships beginning with Captain Cook in 1778. However, exploration is imprinted in their stories as well as their history. It is part of who they are and joining these great ships gave them the opportunity to continue to expand their knowledge of geography and other people and their cultures.

Chapter 5

1   See Chapter 4, note 1, for an explanation on nautical miles.

2   "Grampus" is the genus and another name for Risso's dolphin (*Grampus griseus*) and also another name for the killer whale (*Orcinus orca*). Both can be found in the waters of the Pacific Northwest.

3   He was Chief Tsaxawasip of the Mowachaht tribe of the Nuu-chah-nulth, though Maquinna was the name he was, and still is, most commonly known by.

4   Private trade during the eighteenth century prospered with around 13,000 British and Scottish ships sailing as private enterprises.

5   Captain James Colnett, sailing under the directive of King George's Sound Company, had taken the time and expense of obtaining the proper licensing. He felt the delay made him late arriving at Nootka Sound, by which time Captain Barkley had procured all the furs. Captain Colnett was convinced that Captain Barkley knew he was evading licensing and vowed to put the matter before the EIC upon his return to England.

6   The Chalat', or Hoh, people said they never massacred ship-wrecked sailors. Whatever happened to the crew of the *Imperial Eagle* was an unfortunate event but was not the last such incidence to take place. While Captain Barkley was honourable in his interactions with those he met and traded with, many others who came after were not so disposed and treated Indigenous Peoples with contempt and abuse. It is not surprising that reprisals sometimes took place.

Chapter 6

1   Supercargoes are employed to manage all commercial aspects of the cargo.

2   In 2005, the historic centre of Macau was designated as a UNESCO World Heritage Site.

3   A more accurate rendering of this name would be "Ka'iana." Frances referred to Ka'iana as "Tianna" and would also not have known to include the notation for the glottal stop in his name ('), but I have chosen to use his actual name in the telling of her story. Ka'iana came from the island of Kaua'i. His mother was descended from the ruling houses of O'ahu, Hilo, and Maui. His father was the younger son of Chief Keaweikekahiali'iokamoku of the island of Hawai'i.

4   Ka wahine was a maka'āinana, a commoner, and would not normally have had contact with members of the ali'i (ruling class), but their shared experiences and distance from home most likely created a bond between them.

Chapter 7

1 It is unclear in Frances's diary whether she stayed in Mauritius or went to Calcutta with her husband. She reported that Captain Barkley went to Calcutta and, upon his return, they left Mauritius to sail directly to England. It is most likely that she stayed behind due to her pregnancy.

2 While never recorded, some family stories state the Frances had twins. Ida E. Prosser, whose grandfather was Charles Francis Barkley, Frances' son, wrote a letter that stated, "My brother Cecil Denne wrote to me he had seen the Diary of Mrs. Frances Trevor Barkley, and said the account of the birth of twins on one of the small islands with only an Indian woman to care for her, was very pitiful—one of the babies died." Prosser, I.E., Letter to Constance Parker, March 17, 1934, British Columbia Archives.

Chapter 9

1 The date of their departure was not specified by Frances, but a letter in the East India Company Archives, Fort William-India House Correspondence of April 27, 1792, noted that the *Princess Frederica* left Copenhagen on October 8, 1790.

Chapter 12

1 Old Woman's Island, or Little Colaba, no longer exists. It was originally part of an archipelago of seven islands that, through the process of land reclamation, fused into one to form the city of Mumbai.

Chapter 15

1 The explosion that killed 36,000 people and destroyed two-thirds of the island was still ninety years into the future.

Chapter 16

1 It is impossible to know what his illness was. There were so many diseases that threatened the health of mariners when they sailed in tropical latitudes and very little was understood of the causes.

2 Frances Barkley wrote, "She [Patty] died on board the *Halcyon* on the 15th day of April 1791 or 92." The year was 1792 as that is the year they were in Makassar Strait. Patty died before April 15, as Captain Barkley noted in his log that she was interred on April 5, 1792.

Notes

Chapter 18

1 South Iwo Jima is a volcanic island and is part of the Ogasawara Archipelago. Frances Barkley described it well. It is 913 metres in height with slope of 45 degrees.

Chapter 19

1 In such conditions Captain Barkley would have had to rely on dead reckoning, a method subject to error. The navigator would note the ship's speed and course and track the distance travelled from a previous reading.

Chapter 20

1 It was not until the Tsarist government concluded treaty agreements with England and the United States in 1824 and 1825 that trade was openly welcomed.

Chapter 21

1 Mount St. Elias sits on the border between the Kluane National Park and Reserve in the Yukon and the Wrangell-St. Elias National Park and Preserve in Alaska. Its recoded height is 5,845 metres. The Tlingit name of Yas'éitaa Shaa means "Mountain behind Icy Bay."

2 Mount Fairweather is located on the border between Alaska and western British Columbia in the Fairweather Range of the Saint Elias Mountains. Its recorded elevation is 4,671 metres, making it the highest mountain in British Columbia. It received its European name from Captain Cook for the fair weather he experienced while visiting in 1778.

3 There were few good charts available for use. Perhaps the Barkley's had some knowledge of Captain Cook's charting of the area, but it was sketchy at best. La Pérouse explored the coast in 1786, but his charts were not printed until 1797.

4 Admiralty Bay was named by Captain Nathaniel Portlock during his trip there in 1786, and in the same year Jean-Francois del la Pérouse named it Baie de Monti. Monti Bay today is one of the Bays in the Yakutat Basin. Captain George Dixon (RN) referred to it as Port Mulgrave after the Baron Mulgrave, who was an English Artic explorer.

5 The people they met were most likely Tlingit who inhabited the Yakutat area.

6 The ornament Frances described was a labret, which signaled the status of the women. Slaves, for example, did not have the privilege of wearing a labret. The lip ornament is gradually enlarged until around middle age, when it reaches the size of the bowl of a large tablespoon and extends several inches from the wearer's gums.

7 They most likely anchored in what is now known as Sitka [Shee At'iká in Tlingit], located on the west coast of Baranof Island.

Chapter 22

1   Ka'iana had learned much about the ways of the Europeans during his travels with Meares. He was not quick to surrender to the trivial gifts and ceremony the traders offered. Importantly, he had learned any commitments made to Indigenous Peoples were insincere and transitory and were meant as a bribe in order to gain the commodities the traders were after. He saw all too often that if the traders could not obtain what they wanted through bartering, they would take what they sought by force. Ka'iana was also aware of the significance of his knowledge and power and would use the traders to suit his purposes. Thus, for the Barkleys and other traders, Ka'iana gained a reputation of being less amenable than other Kānaka, and someone to be wary of.

2   Kamehameha was able to obtain muskets from the traders and amassed a great store of them, which helped him in his conquests. After years of war, in 1810, King Kamehameha finally united the Hawaiian Islands under one royal kingdom.

Chapter 23

1   Gia Long (Nguyễn Ánh) was thirty when Frances visited. Although she never came face-to-face with him, she thought him to be a most astounding man, who she said was "indifatigul [sic] in his different occupations." She was referring to his advancement of manufacturing and commercial industry in Saigon, the creation of public schools, the modernization of jurisprudence, and the establishment of a large and powerful navy. In 1804, after many military conquests he became the acknowledged emperor of Vietnam as the sovereign of the country.

Chapter 24

1   Frances did not write in her reminiscences anything about their trip while in Mauritius, but she must have talked to Constance Parker, who was able to retell the story of the Barkleys' time there. I have added information about privateering in the Mauritius and Indian Ocean for historical context.

2   Frances had relayed her story of capture to members of her family and over time a few different versions were told, with the exact location and timing lost to memory. What remained was their release due to her red hair. The timing of their detention likely occurred on their second trip. There were pirates in many places in the world at that time, as there are today, but the most probable place of their hijacking would be somewhere in the South China Sea near the Makassar Strait.

3   Constance Parker's version differs somewhat. Leaving Cochinchina, she thought the Barkleys sailed through the Singapore Strait intending to go to Bombay but were driven too far south due to severe weather conditions. Being ignorant of the

fresh outbreak of hostilities between England and France, they decided to put into Mauritius for food and water. It appears the Barkleys deliberately made their way toward Mauritius. When they came out of the Singapore Strait in late March, they arrived during the inter-monsoon season, when winds are usually light and variable. There were around latitude 1°25'N in an area known as the doldrums. If weather were a factor, it would not affect them until they moved further south to around 10°S, where they could have encountered the last of the cyclone season.

4   The French held on to the Île de France (Mauritius) until they surrendered to British command in 1810.

5   Although they had a safe place to stay while in Port Louis and were protected by their friend's intervention, they were witness to much that was going on regarding the war in that area. It could not have been an easy time for them. It is interesting that Frances never wrote of the specifics during their imprisonment, nor mentioned the large slave trade that was mapped onto the economy of Île de France.

6   On May 5, 1794, the *Princess Royal* (renamed *Duguay Trouin*), now in French hands, was engaged a fierce battle with the British frigate HMS *Orpheus*. For over an hour, the ship sustained multiple blows and was so badly damaged that the French captain eventually struck his colours and surrendered. The Princess Royal had lost twenty men and another sixty who died later from sustained injuries.

7   Frances did not mention the Venus, but a notice from Cox's Island, downriver from Calcutta, reported this incident on December 14, 1793. *A Peoples' History 1793–1844*, "Prizetaking," January 11, 1794, https://houghton.hk, accessed January 2022.

8   The Dutch Governor of Malacca, H. Couperus, *A Peoples' History 1793–1844*, "Prizetaking," Saturday, February 1, 1794, https://houghton.hk, accessed January 2022.

Chapter 25

1   Frances did not say if they sailed north or dropped down toward the Cape Verdi Islands. The northerly route could put them in the path of a mid-Atlantic low-pressure system and adverse winds that time of year, while the southern route, although longer, would give them a more comfortable sail.

Chapter 27

1   This section is compiled from letters and notes written by both Frances and Charles to each other.

2   Charles Barkley, "Letter to John Barkley," ca. 1809, British Columbia Archives.

Epilogue

1 Frances referred to her daughter Martha as "Patty" in honour of the baby that died when they were in Celebes, who was also named Martha but called Patty. She did the same for two of her sons named William: after the first William died, she named a second son William again.

2 Frances did not include anything of her life after her return to England in her book of *Reminiscences,* but she did leave notes and letters from which to draw on. As well, her daughter Martha (Patty) kept a diary in which she fully documented not only her own life, but included updates on her "mamma and papa." Taken together we get snapshots of their remaining years. In keeping with the narrative presented in this book I have continued with the same style of writing using the aforementioned material as the focal point for this part of the story.

Conclusion

1 Upon Captain Charles Barkley's death his son, Charles Frances Barkley, inherited the Halliford house.

2 Fenwick of Lambton, Frances Barkley "Frances' Own Words," https://sites.google.com/site/fenwickoflambton, accessed January 17, 2022.

3 Fenwick of Lambton, "Frances Barkley, Martha Shaw's Journals," First Journal, June 17, 1829, https://sites.google.com/site/fenwickoflambton, accessed January 2022.

4 Dr. Klaus Karttunen, "Shaw, Robert Barkley-Persona of Indian Studies," http://whowaswho-indology.info, accessed January 2022.

Selected Bibliography

Anderson, Captain John. *This Noble Ship*. Victoria, BC Printorium Bookworms/Island Blue, 2016.

Barkley, Charles. *Logbook for the Halcyon and Princess Frederica*. Journal of Proceedings onboard the Brig *Halcyon* and Log of the Ship *Princess Frederica*. British Columbia Archives. AA20.5H12B.

——. *Logbook for the Loudoun*. Journal of the Proceedings onboard the *Loudoun*, 1786–1793. British Columbia Archives. AA20.5L92.

——. "Letter to Frances Barkley from Dublin," May 23, 1808.

——. "Letter to John Barkley from Buenos Aires," 1808. AA30B242. British Columbia Archives.

——. "Letter to Frances Barkley from Bridlington," August 17, 1810.

——. "Letter to Frances Barkley from Cromarty," August 23, 1810.

——. "Letter to Frances Barkley from Cromarty," August 24, 1810.

——. "Letter to Frances Barkley from Cromarty," August 27, 1810.

——. "Letter to Frances Barkley from Cromarty," August 29, 1810.

——. "Letter to Frances Barkley from Edinburgh," September 5, 1810.

"Barkley Family History." Accessed January 26, 2022. https://sites.google.com/site/barkleyfamilyhistory/home.

Barkley, Frances Hornby Trevor. *Frances Barkley's Reminiscences of 1836*. British Columbia Archives. AA30B24.

Barnes, L. Email to Cathy Converse. "Barkley Family," November 7, 2004, May 29, 2018.

Barnes, V. Email to Cathy Converse. "Barkley Family," November 4, 2004.

Barranger, Chelsea. *References to Colonialism, Colonial, and Imperialism: Mauritius Truth Commission*. Centre for Human Rights and Restorative Justice: McMaster University, n.d. https://truthcommissions.huminities.mcmaster.ca.

Battle, Kenneth, "The Halliford House and Asylum," *Journal of the Sunbury and Shepperton Local History Society*, no.77, Autumn 2016: 21–23.

——. "The Barkleys of Halliford House," *Journal of the Sunbury and Shepperton Local History Society*, no. 78, Spring 2017: 21–23.

Broomfield, P. Email to Cathy Converse. "The Barkley's," 2014, 2015, 2021.

Captain Dixon, George. *A Voyage Round the World; but More Particularly to the North-West Coast of America Performed in 1785, 1786, 1787 and 1788, in the King George and Queen Charlotte*. London: Geo. Goulding, 1789.

Chang, David A. *The World and All the Things upon It: Native Hawaiian Geographies of Exploration*. Minneapolis: University of Minnesota Press, 2016.

———. Email to author. "The Barkley's, Winee (Ka Wahine), and Raroia Atoll." March 26, 27, 2014.

Clulow, Adam, and Tristan Mostert, eds. *The Dutch and English East India Companies: Diplomacy, Trade and Violence in Early Modern Asia*. NL Amsterdam: Amsterdam University Press, 2018. https://doi.org/10.5117/9789462983298.

Coles, K Adlard. *Heavy Weather Sailing*. Third. Clinton Corners, New York: John De Graff, Inc., 1981.

Conner, Daniel, and Lorraine Miller. *Master Mariner: Captain James Cook and the Peoples of the Pacific*. Vancouver: Douglas & McIntyre, 1999. https://archive.org/details/mastermarinercapoolorr.

Dalrymple, William. *The Anarchy: The Relentless Rise of the East India Company*. London (GB): Bloomsbury Publishing, 2019.

Earl, Captain. G.E., and Captain E. L. Main. *Munro's Navigation*. Glasgow: James Munro & Co. Ltd., 1952.

"Fenwick of Lambton." Accessed January 2022. sites.google.com/site/fenwickoflambton.

Gough, Barry M. *The Northwest Coast: British Navigation, Trade, and Discoveries to 1812*. Pacific Maritime Studies Series 9. Vancouver: UBC Press, 1992.

Hayes, Derek. *Historical Atlas of the North Pacific Ocean: Maps of Discovery and Scientific Exploration, 1500–2000*. Seattle: Published under the auspices of North Pacific Marine Science Organization [by] Sasquatch Books, 2001.

Hill, Beth. *The Barkley Chair. Westworld Magazine*, 1977.

Hill, Beth, Cathy Converse. *The Remarkable World of Frances Barkley, 1769–1845*. Expanded ed. Surrey, BC; Custer, WA: Touch Wood Editions, 2008.

Houghton, Roger. "'A Peoples' History 1793–1844 from the Newspapers." Accessed January 26, 2022. https://houghton.hk/.

Howay, F. W., Robert Haswell, John Box Hoskins, John Boit, and Columbia, eds. *Voyages of the 'Columbia' to the Northwest Coast, 1787-1790 and 1790-1793*. North Pacific Studies Series, no. 13. Portland, OR: Oregon Historical Society Press in cooperation with the Massachusetts Historical Society, 1990.

Howay, F. W. *The Dixon-Meares Controversy*. Toronto: Ryerson Press, 1929.

Hutchinson, Gillian. "Herman Moll's View of the South Sea Company." *Journal for Maritime Research* 6, no. 1 (December 2004): 87–112. https://doi.org/10.1080/21533 369.2004.9668338.

Kuykendall, Ralph S. "James Colnett and the 'Princess Royal.'" In *The Quarterly of the Oregon Historical Society*, 25:36–52. 1, 1924.

La Salle, Marina. Labrets and Their Social Context in Coastal British Columbia. In *BC Studies*, Winter, 123–53. no. 180. Vancouver: University of British Columbia, 2013.

Lamb, Kate. "The Mystery of Mrs. Barkley's Diary." In *The British Columbia Historical Quarterly*, Vol. VI. no. 1. Victoria, BC: Archives of British Columbia, 1942.

Selected Bibliography

Lindenkohl, Henry. "Rare Maps Collection, Alaska & Polar Regions Collections." In
   Port Mulgrave, Yakutat Bay. 1867–1896. Washington, DC United States Coast Survey
   in 1875, 1875. https://library.uaf.edu/aprca/services/reproductions.
Lloyd's Register of Shipping. 1793. Reprint, Holland: The Gregg Press Limited, 1793. archive.org.
Box People and Places. "Martha Shaw at Middlehill, 1850." Accessed January 26, 2022.
   http://www.boxpeopleandplaces.co.uk/martha-shaw-at-middlehill1850.html.
Massey, Raymond. *Discovery of Hawaii and Honolulu Harbor*. First. Raymond Massey, 2009.
Meares, John. *Voyages Made in the Years 1788 and 1789, from China to the North West
   Coast of America*. London: Logographic Press, 1790.
Meteorological Office. *Meteorology for Mariners*. London: Her Majesty's Stationery
   Office, the Campfield Press, 1956.
Moorhouse, Geoffrey. *Calcutta*. London: Weidenfeld and Nicolson, 1971.
NOAA. "Nautical Charts." *United States Pilot 8 Alaska: Dixon Entrance to Cape Spencer*,
   43rd edition 2021. nauticalcharts.noaa.gov.
Price, A. Grenfell, ed. *The Explorations of Captain James Cook in the Pacific: As Told by
   Selections of His Own Journals 1768–1779*. New York: Dover Publications, 1971.
Sauer, Martin. *An Account of a Geographical & Astronomical Expedition to the
   Northern Parts of Russia...in the Years 1785–1794*. London: A. Straban for T. Cadell
   Jnr. & W. Davies, 1802.
Seton-Karr, Judge of the High Court of Judicature and President of the Record
   Commission, W. S. *Selections from Calcutta Gazetted for the Years 1789–1797
   Showing the Political and Social Condition of the English in India, Seventy Years Ago*.
   Vol. II. Calcutta: Longmans, Green, Reader, and Dyer: Published under the sanction
   of the Government of India, 1865.
Srinivasachari, C. S., ed. *Fort William-India House Correspondence*. IV, XVII vols.
   1764–1766, 1792. Delhi, Civic Lines: East India Company, 1962.
Stanley, H. Email to Cathy Converse. "Frances Barkley," April 13, 15, 2011.
Sutton, Jean. *Lords of the East: The East India Company and its Ships*. London: Conway
   Maritime Press, 1981.
Symes, M. Email to Cathy Converse. *Martha Shaw (Nee Barkley)*, October 1, 2015.
Trevor, A. Email to Cathy Converse. "Frances Trevor Barkley," January 23, 2013.
Unites States Institute of Peace. *Truth Commission: Mauritius*. Vol. 1. United States:
   Government Printing, 2011. https://usip.org.
Utsi, E. Email to Cathy Converse. "Barkley Family," March 4, 9, 11, 2011, May 30, 2011.
"Unveiling of Monuments Erected by Historic Sites and Monuments Board." In *Third
   Annual Report and Proceeding*, 10–16. 1922. Reprint, British Columbia Historical
   Association, 1925.
Walbran, John T. "The Cruise of the Imperial Eagle." In *Victoria Daily Colonist*,
   March 2, 1901.
Wickremerante, S. Email to Cathy Converse. "Frances Barkley," July 22, 2015.

Glossary

Historical Name	Modern Name
Admiralty Bay	Yakutat Bay; Tlingit name: Yaakwdáat Geeyí
Awatcha Bay	Avacha Bay, Russia
Bantam	Banten, Indonesia
Batavia Road	Java, Indonesia
Bay of Le Havre	Baie de Seine
Bocca Tigris	Humen, China
Bombay	Mumbai, India
Calcutta	Kolkata, India
Camoens	Luís de Camões (Portuguese poet)
Canton River	Pearl River or Zhujiang, China
Canton	Guangzhou, China
Cape St. James	Da Nang, Vietnam
Caracasoa Bay	Kealakekua, Hawai'i
Celebes	Sulawesi, Indonesia
Cochinchina	South Vietnam or Đàng Trong
Destruction River	Hoh River or Chalak'ac'it
Dutch East India Company	also known as Verenigde Oostindische Compagnie/voc
Elsinore	Helsingør, Denmark
Friendly Cove	Yuquot, British Columbia
Gelolo	Halmahera island

Glossary

Isle de France	Mauritius
Kakatoire	Krakatoa volcano
Kamskatcha	Kamchatka, Russia
Lord Mulgrave's Harbour	Port Mulgrave
Macao	Macau, China
Madras	Chennai, India
Margion	Makian island
Mount Fairweather	Tlingit name: Tsalxaan
Mount Saint Elias	Tlingit name: Yas'éit'aa Shaa
New Carolina Islands	Caroline Archipelago, also Caroline Islands
Norfolk Sound	Sitka Sound, Alaska
Old Woman's Island	Little Colaba, today part of Mumbai, India
Owyhee	Hawai'i
Olowalu	O'ahu, Hawai'i
Paramocha	Paramushir, Russia
Petropavlovsk	Petropavlovsk-Kamchatsky, Russia
quass	kvass, a type of alcohol
Queen Charlotte Islands	Haida Gwaii
Saigon	Ho Chi Minh City, Vietnam
Sandwich Islands	Hawaiian Archipelago
South Sulphur Island	Minami-Iōtō, formerly known as South Iwo Jima
Spice Islands	Maluku Islands, Indonesia
Sulphur Island	Iō Tō, formerly known as Iwo Jima
Whampoa	Huangpu, China
Whitaty Bay	Waikiki, Hawai'i
Wickaninnish's Sound	Clayoquot Sound, British Columbia

Index

Index

Index

About the Author

CATHY CONVERSE is an award-winning author and historian whose career has spanned more than thirty years. She is the author of *Following the Curve of Time: The Untold Story of Capi Blanchet* and *Against the Current: The Remarkable Life of Agnes Deans Cameron*. For more information, please visit cathyconverse.com.